YALE STUDIES IN ATTITUDE AND COMMUNICATION

Volume 3

EDITED BY CARL I. HOVLAND AND MILTON J. ROSENBERG

YALE STUDIES IN ATTITUDE AND COMMUNICATION

Attitude Organization and Change

AN ANALYSIS OF CONSISTENCY
AMONG ATTITUDE COMPONENTS

BY

Milton J. Rosenberg

Carl I. Hovland

William J. McGuire

Robert P. Abelson

Jack W. Brehm

New Haven and London, Yale University Press

BF
378
.A75A8
(2)

© 1960 by Yale University Press, Inc.
Second printing, December 1963.
Set in Baskerville type
and printed in the United States of America by
The Murray Printing Company, Forge Village, Mass.
All rights reserved. This book may not be
reproduced, in whole or in part, in any form
(except by reviewers for the public press),
without written permission from the publishers.
Library of Congress catalog card number: 60–15892

PREFACE

THE FIRST VOLUME in the Yale Studies in Attitude and Communication presented an experimental analysis of the effects of the organization of persuasive communications upon the degree of attitude change produced. The second volume shifted from this concern with the stimulus aspect of the persuasion transaction toward the kinds of mediating variables commonly classified as personality differences. The present volume attempts to intrude still further into the "interior" of the attitude change process: it reports a series of studies concerned with the consequences of various kinds of changes in the internal organization of attitudes.

While all the studies reported in this volume were conducted within the setting provided by the Yale Communication and Attitude Change Program, they were not undertaken as separate portions of a single and closely coordinated "grand design." Rather, they grew out of a number of quite different approaches to the attitude change process. McGuire and Hovland, starting about 1953, had been concerned with what constitutes inconsistency and how factors influencing it can be measured. This led to McGuire's developing a model based on the syllogism, in which deviations between beliefs regarding the conclusion and beliefs regarding the premises would yield an index of inconsistency and would indicate such tendencies as wishful thinking. Brehm, Janis, and Hovland were concerned with preparatory communications and developed an interest in the conditions under which a *fait accompli*, rather than prior communication, might produce maximal attitude change. Brehm found that

v

this problem could profitably be viewed from the standpoint of "dissonance theory," on which he had done prior research. This led to a series of studies summarized in this volume. In earlier research Rosenberg had investigated the affective and cognitive aspects of stable attitudes. As part of his work in the Yale Program he began to formulate a theoretical view in which the arousal of affective-cognitive inconsistency was assumed to be a necessary condition for the production of attitude change. The studies he reports here have served to test this approach and have also stimulated its further development. Abelson and Rosenberg, who had previously worked on the cognitive mapping of attitudes in their separate research endeavors, shared a joint interest in the relationship among the cognitive elements of affect-laden situations. This led to the development of their model of cognitive consistency processes which was published in 1958, and to the studies and theoretical elaborations which are presented in this volume. As the independent researches developed, seminar discussions indicated that there was much in common in the various studies and that all involved a major concern with factors making for consistent internal organization of attitudes. It then seemed desirable to present these studies in a single monograph so that some of the similarities and differences could be more readily analyzed.

It is noteworthy that in recent years similar interests in the problem of consistency between various components of attitudes and how they are organized and structured have been pursued by many separate investigators. Some of this work is reviewed in our first chapter as well as in subsequent ones. The bases of these interests were various, but whatever they may have been it is clear that the study of attitude dynamics by American social psychologists has shifted in recent years in the direction of consistency models. The present volume is in some ways representative of that shift, and it is our hope that it advances the state of knowledge in such matters to a perceptible degree.

While the separate research chapters present four different theoretical formulations, each attempts to account for attitude change in terms of the arousal and the reduction of inconsistency between affective, cognitive, or behavioral components of attitudes. However, the authors do not assume that the inevitable consequence of inconsistency is its immediate and direct reduction. Quite the contrary, the theoretical formulations they employ, and the experiments they report, are addressed as much to the case in which inconsistency is tolerated or ignored and to the case in which it is reduced without producing general attitude reorganization, as to the case in which its reduction does yield such reorganization. The present formulations are not presented in what is assumed to be their final and definitive statement. Each of the authors is carrying forward further research on closely related problems.

The specific research studies reported in this volume were supported by a number of different organizations and this help is separately acknowledged by each of the authors. Here we should like to express our thanks to the Rockefeller Foundation for its generous support of the Yale Communication and Attitude Change Program as a whole.

We are indebted also to several colleagues whose comments on and criticisms of the original manuscript were of great help to us in preparing this volume for publication. Specifically we tender our thanks to Leonard Doob, Irving L. Janis, Fred D. Sheffield, and Leon Festinger. In no case, however, are they to be held responsible for the contents of the chapters. Mrs. Arlene Skolnick contributed in an important way to the preparation of the summary in Chapter 6 and made helpful editorial suggestions with respect to several other chapters.

Preparation of the manuscript is always a difficult chore. Kristine Christensen, Miriam Strane, and Jane Olejarczyk worked with noteworthy efficiency and frustration tolerance on this phase of the operation. Joyce L. Evans and Grace J. Waite assisted in the task of proofreading. To each we express our deep indebtedness. The Yale University Press was most helpful and co-operative in bringing this volume to completion. Most indispensable was the precise, diligent, and yet highly empathic editing by Jane Olson.

All the studies were conducted while the authors were associated with the Yale Communication and Attitude Change Program. Milton J. Rosenberg, Carl I. Hovland, and Robert P. Abelson are in the Yale Department of Psychology. William J. McGuire and Jack Brehm are now members of the psychology departments of the University of Illinois and Duke University, respectively.

CARL I. HOVLAND
MILTON J. ROSENBERG

New Haven, Conn.
April, 1960

CONTRIBUTORS' ACKNOWLEDGMENTS

VARIOUS PERSONS and institutions have facilitated the separate research endeavors reported in Chapters 2, 3, 4 and 5, respectively. Their contributions are here gratefully acknowledged by the authors of those chapters.

Chapter 2

Useful advice in connection with the earlier study on attitude structure, here briefly reviewed, was provided by Helen Peak. In carrying out the two experiments with which this chapter is mainly concerned, the author has profited from discussions with Robert Abelson, Carl Hovland, and Irving Janis. Philip Zimbardo helped in the execution of the first of these studies and Sheldon Feldman worked long and skillfully in administering the measures used in the second study. Dr. Charles W. Gardner rendered valuable psychiatric consultation on the selection and preparation of the hypnotic subjects. The data analysis phase of the first and all phases of the second study were carried out under contract 609(27) with the Group Psychology Branch of the Office of Naval Research. Special thanks are due Luigi Petrullo and Joan Criswell of that organization for the many ways in which they facilitated the execution of these studies as well as those reported in Chapter 4.

Chapter 3

Valuable help in formulating the hypotheses described in this chapter and in devising methods for testing them was provided by Carl Hovland and Leon Festinger. These studies were also facilitated by financial aid and other resources provided by the Yale Communication and Attitude Change Program, the Social Science Research Council, and the University of Minnesota's Laboratory for Research in Social Relations. Portions of the data reported in this chapter have already appeared in the *Journal of Abnormal and Social Psychology,* 1960, *60,* 345–358.

Chapter 4

In their efforts toward developing a theory of cognitive processes the authors have had valuable stimulation from seminar and other discussions with the following graduate students in the Yale Department of Psychology: Timothy C. Brock, Sheldon Feldman (who also executed a large portion of the statistical analyses reported in this chapter), Jonathan L. Freedman, Sherry F. Israel, David O. Sears, David L. Singer, and Herbert Wells. The experiments reported in this chapter were carried out under contract 609(27) with the Group Psychology Branch of the Office of Naval Research.

Chapter 5

The program of inquiry described in this chapter was carried out while the author was a member of the Communication and Attitude Change Program at Yale University. It was supported by a grant to Carl Hovland from the Bell Telephone Laboratories. The author would like to thank Irving Janis and Edward E. Jones for their various helpful comments and suggestions in regard to preliminary manuscripts of this chapter. Above all he would like to express his indebtedness to Arthur R. Cohen, who has carried at least an equal share of the burden in formulation of many of the ideas and projects reported.

CONTENTS

CHAPTER 1

Cognitive, Affective, and Behavioral Components of Attitudes

MILTON J. ROSENBERG AND CARL I. HOVLAND

ATTITUDES ARE TYPICALLY DEFINED as "predispositions to respond in a particular way toward a specified class of objects." Being predispositions they are not directly observable or measurable. Instead they are inferred from the way we react to particular stimuli. Saying that a man has an unfavorable attitude toward foreigners leads us to expect that he will perceive their actions with distrust, will have strong negative feelings toward them, and will tend to avoid them socially. Thus when attitudes are studied what are observed are the evoking stimuli on the one hand and the various types of response on the other. The types of response that are commonly used as "indices" of attitudes fall in three major categories: cognitive, affective, and behavioral.

For certain types of research it may be sufficient to use a single response as the "index" of an individual's attitude. Thus if we can keep other factors constant and merely introduce some external stimulus, say a communication, we can see how the individual's way of perceiving an issue is changed. For example, if one wants to determine whether presenting a particular point of view in first position, as compared to second position (after the opposing point of view has been presented), produces greater change in attitude, one can administer a scale of verbal statements about the issue before and after the two orders of presentation and compare their impact.

Experiments involving this procedure were described in the first volume of this series (Hovland et al., 1957). These studies yielded results concerning the differences between pro-con and con-pro sequences in modifying *beliefs* about attitude objects. But even in such a situation it is possible that subjects who were similar in their tested beliefs on a particular issue were not similar in how they felt about the issue emotionally or in the actions they would take concerning it.

In nonexperimental situations, uncontrolled variability in the factors that influence attitudinal responses makes for still greater uncertainty. Thus, despite the fact that two persons respond in the same way on one specific index of attitude (say, how they vote on a school bond proposal) they may hold very different beliefs, expectations, feelings, and action orientations toward the matter at issue. Indeed if attitude is defined as the *set* of "predispositions to respond in a particular way toward some particular class of stimuli," they may hold quite different *attitudes*. On the other hand, it is quite conceivable that for a given person, or group of persons, or for a given issue, the various types of indices by which "attitudes" are estimated may be highly and predictably related to one another. This is assumed when, frequently, we infer one type of response from another.

These considerations reflect a major problem in attitude measurement and theory: the relationship between the three major components of attitude and the factors which increase or decrease their correlation. It is to this problem that the present volume is addressed.

In the accompanying diagram our formulation is presented in simple schematic form. We here indicate that attitudes are predispositions to respond to some class of stimuli with certain classes of responses and designate the three major types of response as cognitive, affective, and behavioral. Attention to these different aspects of attitude goes back at least to McDougall (1908) and persists in current work (cf. the interesting discussion by Katz and Stotland, 1959). To a

Figure 1. Schematic Conception of Attitudes

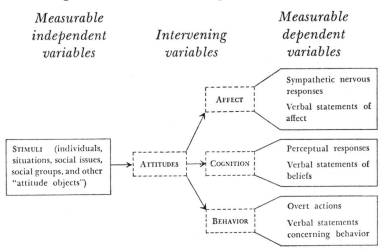

large extent these response classes are themselves abstractions or constructs and are typically inferred from the specific types of measurable response indicated at the extreme right. Thus an individual's affective response toward another individual may be inferred from measures of such physiological variables as blood pressure or galvanic response (cf. Lawson and Stagner, 1957), but is more typically inferred from verbal statements of how much he likes or dislikes him. Similarly how an individual will *act* toward a given situation may be evaluated by how he does respond when directly confronted with the situation but may also be inferred from what he says he will do in the given situation. *Cognitions* include perceptions, concepts, and beliefs about the attitude object and these are usually elicited by verbal questions in printed or oral form.

The basic question in studies of attitude dynamics is how, or under what conditions, responses in any or all of these three classes undergo relatively persisting alteration. This question can be pursued in various ways. The first volume in the present series, *The Order of Presentation in Persuasion,* was mainly concerned with the patterning of communications intended to alter attitudes. The second volume, *Personality and Persuasibility,* investigated certain personality characteristics that seem to foster general receptivity to such communications. The present volume, by focusing on factors influencing the correlation between different types of response components, represents a third approach; one in which attitude change is related to the internal *organization* of attitudes.

Considerable research and theorizing have been directed toward the analysis of each of the three attitude components of interest to us—cognitive, affective, and behavioral. The cognitive component has received considerable emphasis during the last two decades. The study by Katz and Braly (1933) was an early attempt to investigate the cognitive content of attitudes. A well-known finding from this study was that prejudiced respondents were markedly similar in the "traits" they attributed to members of disliked ethnic groups. Harding et al. (1954) have reviewed a number of studies in which the procedures developed by Katz and Braly were used to study cognitive stereotypes associated with prejudices.

Another cognitive aspect of attitude was investigated by

Hartley (1946) and Kramer (1949). In both these studies it was shown that groups perceived with varying degrees of clarity may elicit equally hostile attitudes.

In another group of studies some dimensions upon which the cognitive components of attitudes are likely to vary have been investigated. Thus Axelrod (1959), Carlson (1956), Nowlis (1960), Peak (1959), Rosenberg (1956), Smith (1949), and Woodruff (1942) have reported studies in which beliefs about relations between attitude objects and goal states have been singled out for special attention. These and other dimensions of beliefs about attitude objects have been discussed in theoretical articles by a number of writers, among whom are Abelson and Rosenberg (1958), Cartwright and Harary (1956), Heider (1946), Katz and Stotland (1959), Peak (1958), and Tolman (1951). Similarly the studies by Osgood and his associates (1958), employing the "semantic differential" technique, may be interpreted as illuminating some of the major cognitive dimensions of attitudes.

For the majority of researchers, however, evaluation of the affective component has been central. The attitude scales developed by Thurstone (1929) were primarily intended as evaluations of the respondent's feeling about the object or issue of concern. Krech and Crutchfield (1948) have stressed the importance of feelings of being "for or against" something and having "positive or negative affect" in distinguishing attitudes from opinions. Consistent with this emphasis, the bulk of attitude research, whether undertaken by "pollsters" or by experimenters, has involved some index of "affect" (or "evaluative response") as the prime measure of attitude. Extensive documentation of this point is available in the reviews by Green (1954), Harding et al. (1954), and Hovland (1954).

A few experimental studies have been reported in which classical conditioning procedures have been employed to generate attitudelike emotional responses toward previously neutral stimuli. Thus Lazarus and McLeary (1951) have shown that subjects respond emotionally (i.e. "autonomically") to subthreshold presentations of nonsense syllables that have been paired with electric shock. The experiments by Statts and Statts (1958, 1959) are probably more pertinent to the study of attitudes. A typical finding in these studies is that stimulus words that have been paired with emotionally toned words tend to shift in their locations on the evaluative dimension isolated by Osgood's semantic differential technique.

Of the three major types of attitudinal response delineated in our diagramatic scheme, "overt behavior" has perhaps received the least amount of systematic study and has been least often used as the main index of attitude. But a few studies, among which are those of Cartwright (1949), Katz and Kahn (1952), La Pierre (1934), and Schanck (1932), have been reported in which attitudes are characterized through some index of overt behavior. In these studies, however, the data force the conclusion that overt action toward an object reflects not only the attitude elicited by that object but also the influence of other variables.

While all of the research studies described above stress a particular response component of attitude, some of them, particularly those concerned with the cognitive aspect, also deal with the problem of the *interrelation* of the various classes of attitudinal response. It is the purpose of the present volume to pursue this problem further. Thus each of the present studies is directly oriented toward some major aspect of the interrelation and interaction between the classes of response associated with attitude.

Before turning to the present group of studies, however, it will be useful to ask what kinds of studies have been undertaken, and what kinds of conclusions reached, in earlier work along similar lines.

Perhaps the most common approach in previous research has been that involving correlational study of the separate response components of attitudes. Thus, to cite two examples: Stouffer (1931) has investigated the relationship between behavior and attitude scales; and Lund (1925) has dealt with the correlation between beliefs and desires. A systematic review of many of the early studies of this type will be found in the pre-war survey by Murphy, Murphy, and Newcomb (1937).

The phenomena of attitude change have also been investigated by means of correlational procedures. Some outstanding examples are the study by Newcomb (1943) on changes in attitude during college years and the studies by Lazarsfeld and his colleagues (1944) on voting behavior. In such studies the separate response components of attitude are investigated not only for their relationships to one another but also for the influence of background variables upon those relationships.

Studies of this type have yielded many valuable findings; but at the same time the nature of the correlational method sets limits upon the theoretical significance of the data. Thus without control over the general setting in which the data are collected the influence of other variables upon the obtained findings is not easily assessed. Nor is it always possible to draw conclusions about the causal relationships represented in such data.

A second method has been one utilizing "case histories" to investigate the correlation between attitude components and to study the relationships between attitude and aspects of personal history or personality. Illustrations of this approach are the early study by Murray and Morgan (1945) and more recently studies by Adorno, Frenkel-Brunswik, and colleagues (1950) and by Smith, Bruner, and White (1956). In general such studies have suggested some ways in which the person's social attitudes (and the interrelation between their components) may be influenced and shaped by his major emotional needs, conflicts, and defense mechanisms. Taken together such studies yield broad and dramatic "clinical" findings in which social attitudes are pulled out of the limbo to which social psychologists too often relegate them and are incorporated into the general pattern of integrated psychological processes that are summarized in the term "personality."

But to the extent that one aspires toward reductionist analysis and toward precise delineation of the variables influencing the relations between attitude responses such findings cannot be fully satisfying. The problem must be pursued through procedures that enable close control over interacting, independent variables and close measurement of dependent variables. Experimental methods are required for this purpose and this is the principal methodology employed in the present studies.

Experimentation typically involves controlled manipulation of some variable and estimation of related change in some other variable. Thus most experimental work bearing on the interrelation of attitude components has comprised attempts to produce "attitude change." Attitude change experiments have dealt with a wide range of variables and hypotheses, but until fairly recent times these have been mainly concerned with the impact of the change-inducing communication or with aspects of the situation in which the communication has been received. More recently a number of experiments have been reported in which attention is focused on the production of inconsistency between response components and its consequences with regard to the ultimate reorganization of the attitudes to which these components refer.

A general and frequently replicated finding obtained in some of these studies is the simple one that persons are more satisfied by "consistent" arrangements of related responses than by "inconsistent" arrangements. Among the large number of studies demonstrating this cardinal fact are those by Burdick and Burns (1958), Esch (in Heider, 1958), Horowitz, Lyons, and Perlmutter (1951), Jordan (1953), and Kogan and Taguirri (1958). Some, but not all, of these studies seem, however, to be restricted to mere demonstration. By arousing quite intense and extreme discrepancies between responses referring to the same object they usually succeed in eliciting attempts to reduce inconsistency; however, the extents, limits, and complexities of the general phenomenon are not illuminated.

In addition to those studies mainly concerned with demonstrating the preference for consistency there are a number that are oriented toward the exposition and development of the detailed propositions of various theories concerned with response consistency. These include studies based on Festinger's "dissonance theory" (1957), Heider's theory of "interpersonal perception" (1946, 1958), Newcomb's theory of "communicative acts" (1953, 1959), and Osgood and Tannenbaum's "congruity" approach (1955). Neither the concepts and hypotheses which make up these separate theories, nor the experiments intended to test them, will be reviewed here; where pertinent they will be discussed in subsequent chapters.

The studies in the present volume seek to clarify and extend some of the issues raised in earlier investigations; particularly they seek to examine these issues in ways that contribute to our general understanding of the processes involved in attitude change. Two types of general questions are posed which seem to combine a number of important theoretical issues. The first is an examination of the common hypothesis that affective and behavioral changes will result from exposure to verbal stimuli which change one's conception and perception of the object of the communication. Since attitudes also have both affective and behavioral components this hypothesis amounts to an assumption that affect and behavior components are modified as a result of changes in the cognitive components. Indeed there is some research by Carlson (1956), Peak (1959), Woodruff and DiVesta (1948), and others indicating that this process occurs. What then is the nature of the other linkages between the components? Are cognitions changed when the affect toward the attitude object is modified? Is affect modified when behavior change is induced? What is the influence of "contextual" or "structural" factors? These are some of the questions to which the present volume is addressed.

Closely related is another assumption made in persuasive communication, namely that when the communicator is able to present evidence indicating the need to change one of one's premises, there will be a corresponding change in the conclusion that will be drawn. Thus if the recipient believes a civic improvement is undesirable because it will be too costly, the communicator often takes as his task the demonstration that the improvement will not be too costly and assumes that the recipient will then modify his opinion of the desirability of the proposed construction as a result. Does this in fact happen and if so how is the process mediated? This is a second type of question whose answer is sought in the present studies.

All the studies reported make use of the same sort of research strategy. Typically the relationships between a number of attitude components are measured in a complex setting before any communication or other manipulation is presented. Then one group is systematically exposed to devices designed to change one of the attitude components while a second similar group either is kept as a control or exposed to some other manipulation. Then the changes in each group are compared. This permits an analysis of the complex patterns of changes among the various components as a result of modification of the single component which is being influenced by the communication or other agency of change.

Each of the studies reported seeks to test and extend a particular theoretical orientation concerned with response consistency and attitude dynamics. But no common theoretical position is involved. While the theoretical constructions advanced in two of these chapters (the one by Rosenberg and the one by Rosenberg and Abelson) have much in common, their theoretical positions differ considerably from those by McGuire and by Brehm. Similarly the latter two chapters differ considerably from each other.

It should be clear when these chapters have been read that the differences are not necessarily disagreements. Indeed it seems to us more accurate to view the differences (or better, the contrasts) between the contributions as due to the fact that each is an attempt to test and develop a particular model. Believing that the current state of attitude theory permits no one available model to be judged clearly preferable to all others, the authors have not attempted to employ a completely uniform vocabulary or uniform set of concepts. Each chapter pursues a particular and special way of formally casting up some of the general issues that have been raised in this introduction. A brief preview of the approaches and issues dealt with in each chapter may be helpful.

Rosenberg attempts to elaborate a theoretical scheme of attitude change that is related to his earlier work on attitude structure (1953, 1956). In this earlier work, some portions of which he reviews, it was demonstrated that the affective and cognitive components of attitudes are ordinarily organized in congruence with one another. His present contribution is based on ·the postulate that the disruption of affective-cognitive congruence by alteration of *either* of the two components sets in motion processes of congruence restoration which will, under certain conditions, lead to attitude reorganization through complementary change in the previously unaltered component.

The two experiments he reports are offered to demonstrate, and elaborate upon, the possibility that change in the affective aspect of an attitude does, under certain conditions, generate corresponding change in its cognitive portion. In the final section of his chapter he attempts to develop, on the basis of these and other data, a "two-sequence" model of the attitude change process. He attempts also to specify some conditions under which these sequences will be more or less likely to occur.

The theoretical formulation offered by McGuire pursues the question of response interrelation in a conceptual setting provided by the structure of the formal logic syllogism. Its major proposition is the familiar one that if made aware of inconsistencies inherent in his present beliefs and evaluations, a person will tend to alter these beliefs and evaluations toward greater consistency. In the specific terms of McGuire's theory this proposition is exemplified by a person's changing his degree of acceptance of a syllogistic conclusion so as to bring it into congruence with his separate evaluations of the "probabilities" of its major and minor premises.

But McGuire does not assume that loyalty to the canons of logic is an unopposed motivational force. On the contrary, his theoretical model posits a tendency toward "wishful thinking" which, depending upon its strength with regard to a particular set of propositions, may operate so as to reduce and interfere with the tendency toward "logical" organization of syllogistic premises and conclusions. The experiments reported were undertaken to test a number of derived hypotheses concerned with the effects of the interaction between the assumed preference for consistency and the assumed tendency toward wishful thinking. The results of these experiments are in the main consistent with the original hypotheses and are interpreted by McGuire as arguing for a trend to achieve and maintain "consistency between belief and desire." In the last section of his chapter McGuire examines his own findings and those of earlier researchers for what they seem to reveal about the sources of inconsistency between related beliefs.

The chapter by Rosenberg and Abelson is directly continuous with an earlier theoretical article (1958) in which they presented "A Model of Attitudinal Cognition." In both this earlier article and in their present chapter these authors attempt an approach to the *structure* of attitude in which a balance principle similar to that used in Heider's theory of interpersonal perception is employed. A number of similarities and differences between their approach and Heider's are detailed.

Two experiments are reported which confirm some aspects of their earlier formulation; the second also suggests the need for modification of the original model so as to encompass "gain-seeking" motivation. This pattern of motivation is represented as one which, under certain conditions, operates in opposition to the motivation for cognitive balance. In the last section of their chapter these authors present a more detailed and more "microscopic" set of hypotheses about the processes assumed to underlie the achievement of "balance" in previously imbalanced "attitudinal cognitions."

Brehm utilizes Festinger's "Dissonance Theory" as a source of hypotheses about consistency. He is particularly concerned with the situation in which the person engages in an act that, by its nature, violates some of his motivations and convictions. He develops a number of generalizations as to factors influencing changes in cognitions when behavior is modified.

A number of specific questions are asked about the operation of the dissonance-reduction process when behavior opposite to one's convictions and motivations is induced. One of these questions is whether the mere *commitment* to execute a "dissonant" act, as distinguished from *actual* execution, is a sufficient condition for change in attitude toward the referent of that act. Another major question raised by Brehm is whether the execution of a disliked act will result in a change in one's affects and beliefs toward it only when such execution is "freely" chosen or also when it is "forced" upon the person.

In summary then, the four research reports presented in this volume have a number of things in common. Each attempts through manipulative, experimental procedures to test and extend a particular theoretical formulation of the processes involved in attitude dynamics. While different from one another in the styles and levels of theoretical analysis that they represent, each of the formulations is focused on the question of how, and under what conditions, individuals respond to the introduction of inconsistency between the separate response components of their attitudes. Typically the experimental studies reported in this volume have attempted to arouse and measure such inconsistencies, and the subjects' responses to them, with methods that encompass the structural context in which the inconsistencies are embedded. The researches do not concentrate on individual differences in response to inconsistency. However, the authors are concerned with this issue and, at a number of points in the research chapters and in the concluding chapter, do address themselves to it.

CHAPTER 2

An Analysis of Affective-Cognitive Consistency

MILTON J. ROSENBERG

IN THE FIRST CHAPTER attitudes have been conceptualized as usually featuring consistency between the feelings, beliefs, and overt actions elicited by their objects. Since overt actions are guided by underlying affective and cognitive responses, as well as by situational restrictions, one way of conveniently narrowing the study of response consistency in stable and changing attitudes is to investigate the correspondence between their affective and cognitive components. In the present chapter some propositions suggested by correlational studies of these components are formulated and some manipulative experiments designed to test these propositions are reported.

BACKGROUND

In recent years a few contributions have appeared which, by examining the affective-cognitive organization of attitudes, have pointed the way toward the development of a general theory of attitude structure. One such contribution was the systematic formulation by Krech and Crutchfield (1948). Their definition of attitude is well known: "an enduring organization of motivational, emotional, perceptual and cognitive processes with respect to some aspect of the individual's world." Various other writers have helped to sharpen this sort of approach by emphasizing the concept of *value* and by suggesting that the cognitive aspect of a person's attitude may consist largely of expectations about how his values are served through the agency of the attitude object (Chein, 1948; French, 1947; Heider, 1946; Hilliard, 1950; Peak, 1955; Tolman, 1951).

During the past fifteen years various empirical studies have appeared in which the individual's affective disposition toward an object was related to his beliefs about its value-attaining powers. One of the earliest and most provocative was that by Smith (1949). A major finding was that the extent of positive or negative feeeling toward the Soviet Union could be predicted from the person's pattern of values and his beliefs about how these values are "engaged" (influenced) by the Soviet Union. Cartwright (1949) reported parallel findings with regard to attitudes toward purchase of war bonds (as reflected in actual purchasing behavior), and Woodruff (1942) and Woodruff and DiVesta (1948) reported a series of similar studies on attitudes toward educational issues.

For each of these authors two aspects of the "means-end" cognition stand out: (1) the importance of the value (i.e. its "intensity") and (2) the certainty or strength of the attitude object's relation to that value.

In general, these studies demonstrated that an attitude could be understood as a relatively stable constellation of affective and cognitive responses toward an "object" rather than as a mere affective set. But three separate deficiencies are apparent when these studies are subjected to closer scrutiny. The first, as is almost inevitable in any venture into new territory, is simply that the measurement of the cognitive aspects of attitudes is undertaken rather crudely. Cartwright, relying primarily upon interview data, is able to quantify only on a rather gross scale; inter-subject and intra-subject variation, both in the intensity with which values are held and the certainty with which they are seen as affected by "buying war bonds," is probably more finely graded than the set of coding categories to which such matters are reduced. The studies of Smith and Woodruff are marked by a similar limitation, and although the latter employs rating scales, the number of values with which the subjects work is so small as to prevent their revealing their cognitive structures in full detail.

A second deficiency in this body of work is that, except for the experiment by Woodruff and DiVesta (1948), all of the studies in question are correlational rather than manipulative. Thus they demonstrate the presence of consistency between affects and beliefs but they contribute no data concerning how affective-cognitive structures come to be organized and how permanent alterations are effected.

Perhaps because of this very limitation these researchers tended at the time they reported their studies (both Cartwright and Smith have since reported more complex approaches to problems of attitude structure: Cartwright and Harary, 1956; Smith, Bruner, and White, 1956) to view attitude learning and attitude change as primarily due to changes in beliefs about attitude objects, while they tended to ignore the possibility that these effects might also be produced through other and less "rational" processes.

With the first of these three points in mind the present author undertook a study (Rosenberg, 1953, 1956) which attempted to use more comprehensive measurement of the cognitive components of attitudes. The principal hypothesis was: *When a person has a relatively stable tendency to respond to a given object with either positive or negative affect, such a tendency is accompanied by a cognitive structure made up of beliefs about the potentialities of that object for attaining or blocking the realization of valued states; the sign (positive or negative) and extremity of the affect felt toward the object are correlated with the content of its associated cognitive structure.* Thus strong and stable positive affect toward a given object should be associated with beliefs that it leads to the attainment of a number of important values, while strong negative affect should be associated with beliefs that the object tends to block the attainment of important values. Similarly, moderate positive or negative affects should be associated with beliefs that relate the attitude object either to less important values or, if to important values, then with less confidence about the relationships between these values and the attitude object.

In testing the hypothesis the following experiment was carried out. One hundred and seventeen undergraduate subjects were given an attitude questionnaire dealing with the issue of "whether members of the Communist party should be allowed to address the public." Each subject checked his first choice among five alternative statements. This questionnaire served as a measure of attitudinal affect.

Three to five weeks after the administration of the attitude measure a test of cognitive structure was administered individually. Since this test device was also employed in the two studies reported in the next section of this chapter it will be described in detail. The subject was required to categorize each of a group of value items in terms of (1) *value importance,* i.e. its importance to him as a "source of satisfaction," and (2) *perceived instrumentality* (of the attitude object for the attainment of the value in question), i.e. his estimate as to whether and to what extent that value would tend to be achieved or blocked through the "policy of allowing members of the Communist party to address the public."

The test of cognitive structure utilized a set of 35 value

cards based on White's (1951) value-analysis technique and
Murray's (1938) analysis of major needs, as well as some
values derived from each subject's own previous responses.
For most subjects the total number of such "salient" values
came to two or three, the range among all subjects extending
from zero to six.

For the "value importance" measure the subject was asked
to place each card on a 21-category scale to indicate how much
satisfaction he gets, or would get, from the value state it described. The categories ranged from "gives me maximum
satisfaction" (category $+10$) through "gives me neither satisfaction nor dissatisfaction" (category 0) to "gives me maximum dissatisfaction" (category -10). The intermediate categories on either side of category 0 represented intermediate
degrees of satisfaction and dissatisfaction. For the measure
of "perceived instrumentality" he was asked to rate each
card on an 11-category scale. Category $+5$ represented "complete attainment" of the value through the agency of "Com-
munists being allowed to address the public." Category 0
represented "neither attainment nor blocking" and category
-5 represented "complete blocking." Again the intermediate categories on either side of 0 represented intermediate
degrees of variation. Both the affective and cognitive measures
had good test-retest reliability (Rosenberg, 1956).

The main index used for evaluation was obtained by al-
gebraically summing the importance-instrumentality products for each of the values. Thus when a positive value
(rated, say, as $+7$ in its capacity to satisfy the subject) was perceived as being attained through the policy of allowing members of the Communist party to address the public (to the
extent, say, of a rating of $+3$ on "instrumentality"), the
product was $+21$. If on the other hand, the same value were
rated as being *blocked* by the policy of allowing members of
the Communist party to address the public (for example, a

rating of —3 on "instrumentality") the resultant product would have been —21. Similarly, a value rated as yielding dissatisfaction and thus bearing a minus sign on "value importance" would yield a negative product if multiplied by a rating of positive instrumentality and a positive product if multiplied by a rating of negative instrumentality. The single algebraic quantity obtained by summing all such products represented the total import of the subject's pattern of beliefs about the attitude object's value-attaining and value-blocking powers.

TABLE 1. *Some relationships between attitudinal affect and attitudinal cognition (from Rosenberg, 1956)*

Cognitive index against which index of attitudinal affect is cross-classified	Chi square	p
Algebraic sum of importance-instrumentality products for all value items	26.33	$<.001$
Algebraic sum of the instrumentality ratings of the values ranking 1–10 in importance	20.82	$<.01$
Algebraic sum of the importance ratings of the values ranking 1–5 on positive instrumentality (attainment of values)	12.75	$<.05$

A major finding (reproduced in Table 1) indicates that this index of cognitive structure is quite significantly related to the measure of additudinal affect. In sign (positive or negative) and magnitude the scores on the index of cognitive structure are clearly associated with the subjects' affective responses toward the attitude object. Similar indices, varying from the present one only in the group of values from which they are calculated, yielded similar findings. Thus the data strongly supported the hypothesis that beliefs associated with an attitudinal affect tend to be congruent with it.

While this finding confirmed the existence of a relationship between a measure of affect toward an object and a measure based upon both the "importance" of values and "perceived instrumentality" of the attitude object for attaining those values, the question remained whether each of these variables could be demonstrated to covary with affect when the other is held constant. Employing an index (see Rosenberg, 1956) which reflects variation in perceived instrumentality while value intensity is held constant, it is found (see Table 1) that perceived instrumentality is significantly related to the measure of attitudinal affect. Where the index value is negative the related affect score is negative; where it is positive the related affect score is positive. The size of the index value is positively related to the extremity of the affect score. Conversely a relationship between value importance and attitudinal affect was obtained under the condition in which perceived instrumentality was held constant. Thus extreme attitudinal affects are associated with values of high importance while moderate attitudinal affects are associated with values of less importance.

While this study confirmed and extended the findings of the earlier studies by Cartwright, Smith, and Woodruff, it did not go beyond the limits inherent in correlational research. To test certain dynamic propositions which seem to follow from these "static" data two further studies were undertaken in which experimental manipulations were employed. In the next section these experiments and the theoretical formulation to which they relate are described.

RESEARCH EVIDENCE

Data such as those just reviewed, although "ahistorical," suggest that the attitude change process might be conceived in terms of the arousal and reduction of affective-cognitive inconsistency. It is probably on this basis that some of the authors mentioned above have suggested that the modification of a person's beliefs about the gain yield associated with an attitude object will generate change in his evaluation of that object. Clearly there is much evidence from "applied" fields like advertising that such a pattern of attitude change does occur. But other evidence, such as that on "prestige suggestion" and on conformity to group pressures, suggests that this simple formulation is inadequate; it does not encompass the total range of phenomena which would have to be explained by a general theory of attitude change.

The present formulation is intended to meet this lack by incorporating the demonstrated fact that attitudes feature affective-cognitive consistency into a "homeostatic" conception of attitude dynamics. The cardinal proposition in the present approach is that: *When the affective and cognitive components of an attitude are mutually consistent the attitude is in a stable state; when the affective and cognitive components are mutually inconsistent (to a degree that exceeds the individual's present tolerance for such inconsistency) the attitude is in an unstable state and will undergo spontaneous reorganizing activity until such activity eventuates in either (1) the attainment of affective-cognitive consistency or (2) the placing of an "irreconcilable" inconsistency beyond the range of active awareness.*

The concept "tolerance for inconsistency" requires some elaboration. It is not assumed that *any* degree, however slight, of affective-cognitive inconsistency will be sufficient to motivate the individual. What is assumed is that for any particular attitude as held by any particular person there is some limit to the degree of inconsistency that he will be able to tolerate. If this limit, which may be conceived as an "intolerance-for-inconsistency threshold," is exceeded the attitude will then be rendered unstable and the relationships posited in the proposition will then become operative. (In the remainder of this chapter this qualifying condition is assumed, though not necessarily restated, whenever the proposition given above or data bearing upon it are discussed.) Of the two possible outcomes of intolerable affective-cognitive inconsistency the second is a special, but important, case: as stated it is meant to encompass the possibility that repression or deverbalization may be brought into play in dealing with inconsistencies that, because of the strength of the forces or "facts" that maintain them, as in deep-rooted personality conflicts, for example, do not admit of reduction or resolution. The first possibility is the one with which this chapter is largely concerned; it is assumed that this outcome is the more common of the two when social attitudes are involved.

Thus when affective-cognitive inconsistency in a social attitude is due to initial cognitive changes it would be predicted, from the general proposition given above, that if these changes were "irreversible," the person's related affect would undergo corresponding change. It has been pointed out that just such a process is frequently assumed to underlie attitude change effects. To demonstrate, however, as our major proposition asserts, that affective-cognitive inconsistency (rather than mere cognitive reorganization) is an underlying condition for attitude change, the reverse prediction would also have to be confirmed: it would have to be shown that the production of an irreversible *affect* change will generate corresponding cognitive change in the consistency-restoring direction.

Of these two predictive hypotheses there is much clearer and stronger evidence for the former than for the latter. Thus, in addition to evidence from applied areas, there are literally scores of studies in which communications designed to change means-end cognitions are directed at subjects. (For reviews of such "communication and persuasion" studies, see Murphy, Murphy, and Newcomb, 1937; Doob, 1948; Hovland, 1954; Harding et al., 1954.)

A result found in the vast number of these studies is that

such communications, if potent enough, do produce further change effects in evaluative (affective) responses. Most of the studies, however, do not provide for a precise check of whether, and to what extent, the communications designed to alter cognitions actually do so. At least two studies have been reported in which instrumentality changes producing affect change are measured and demonstrated (the aforementioned one by Woodruff and DiVesta, 1948; and Carlson, 1956). Similarly, a recent study by Peak (1959) demonstrates the same point with reference to the value intensity aspect of cognitive structure. Taken together these three studies, though they were not undertaken to test the present theoretical formulation, do provide strong support for the first of the two predictions derived from it.

When one seeks comparable evidence in support of the hypothesis that inconsistency based on *affect change* will be reduced by cognitive reorganization, the experimental literature provides few relevant studies. Yet included in many of the change-inducing procedures that have been reported are techniques which seem to operate through direct modification of affective responses or, at least, of affect-expressing behavior. A similar impression is generated by an examination of "real life" examples of "irrational" persuasion techniques.

It was with the intention of disentangling affect modification from contexts in which its effects are difficult to trace that the studies reported in the remainder of this paper were undertaken. The specific aim was to put to strict experimental test the second of the two hypotheses derived from the guiding proposition that persons strive to reduce affective-cognitive inconsistency within an attitude structure.

Thus it was specifically predicted that *the strong and irreversible alteration of an attitudinal affect would eventuate in reorganization of the person's associated cognitions.*

COGNITIVE REORGANIZATION IN
RESPONSE TO THE EXPERIMENTAL
MANIPULATION OF ATTITUDINAL AFFECT

The most important requirement for testing the cognitive consequences of affect change is an affect manipulation which is as "pure" (i.e. as unmixed with cognitive assertions) as possible. While "real life" experience does provide reinforcement schedules that act directly to change previously stable affects, few analogous experimental operations are readily available. The one operation that seemed most promising was hypnotic suggestion. Thus in the experiment reported immediately below, posthypnotic suggestions designed to change attitudinal affects were employed.

Method

Eleven deeply "hypnotizable" subjects were drawn from a group recruited in Yale's professional and graduate schools. After a few hypnotic practice sessions, each of the subjects was able to achieve consistently the kind of hypnosis which enabled him to execute posthypnotic suggestions while having amnesia for the fact that such suggestions were given. These eleven subjects were assigned to an experimental group in which each subject was to receive posthypnotic suggestions of affect change toward certain objects.

Eleven other subjects were assigned to a control group which was to undergo all the testing procedures used with the experimental group except the posthypnotic suggestions of affect change. The scarcity of "perfect" hypnotic subjects made it impossible to assign any to the control group; but all the control subjects, while not capable of consistent achievement of posthypnotic amnesia, were capable at least of attaining the level of hypnosis in which classic sensory-motor phenomena are regularly obtained, and some were capable of still deeper levels.

In the first phase of the experiment each subject was given an attitude questionnaire designed to measure his affective responses toward seven different social issues and also requiring him to rate these issues from most to least interesting. For each issue a modified Coombs (1952) scaling procedure was used which generates sixteen scale positions running from extreme positive affect to extreme negative affect. The seven issues used were: labor's right to strike, the city-manager plan, the United States being more conciliatory toward Russia, the provision of comprehensive Federal medical insurance, living in Los Angeles, Negroes moving into white neighborhoods, and the United States and Canada uniting to form a single nation.

Either one week (for six of the subjects in each group) or two weeks (for the remaining five in each group) later each subject was run through a final session. At this time his cognitive structure for one of his two high-interest attitude areas [1] was tested twice, once before and once after a half-hour interval during which he was hypnotized and given a suggestion of affect change for that attitude area. The control subjects merely rested in an identical physical setting after being instructed to "try to fall asleep."

Whatever the specific issues, all the posthypnotic suggestions followed the same form. Thus one representative experimental subject was told:

> When you awake you will be very much in favor of Negroes moving into white neighborhoods. The mere idea of Negroes moving into white neighborhoods will give you a happy, exhilarated feeling. Although you will not remember this suggestion having been made, it

1. All the procedures described in this section were also used for each subject in connection with one of his two *low-interest* attitude areas. The findings based upon these data replicate those reported here. For the complete results of this experiment see Rosenberg, 1960.

will strongly influence your feelings after you have awakened. Only when the signal to remember is given will you remember . . . and only then will your feelings revert to normal.

Whatever actual attitude issue was used, all subjects received posthypnotic suggestions in this form. It should be noted that the subject is simply commanded to *feel* differently toward the attitude object but is not told to change any of his related beliefs. For six of the experimental subjects the affective manipulation was from negative to positive and for the remaining five, from positive to negative. Upon awakening from hypnosis each subject once again filled out the questionnaire measure of affect, and following this the cognitive structure test was readministered.

The hypnotic subjects were told a cover story to the effect that they were participating in two separate experiments; all tests were administered by a person other than the hypnotist. Post-experimental questioning indicated that none of the hypnotic subjects had suspected any connection between the hypnotic and testing sessions.

The technique for measuring cognitive structure was essentially the same as that employed in the study described above, but involved a revised group of 31 value terms. The subject was required to rate each value for the degree of satisfaction or dissatisfaction it afforded him (value importance) and for the extent to which, as the subject saw it, that value would be attained or blocked via the instrumental effects of the attitude object (perceived instrumentality). Again, the use of this device enabled the computation of an "index of cognitive structure" obtained by determining the algebraic sum of the separate importance-instrumentality products.

Results

The comparability of the experimental and control groups.
The question was raised whether the fact that the two groups
of subjects were not equated for "hypnotizability" might have
confounded the experimental design. It could be argued
that because of some untested personality correlates of hypnotizability the experimental group members might have
greater attitudinal instability than the control group members.

To check against this possibility the two groups were compared on the affect change scores (from pre-test to post-test)
of their members. When the hypnotic subjects' mean affect
change scores (based upon the five attitude areas that were
not manipulated) are ranked together with control subjects'
comparable mean affect change scores the chance probability of the obtained difference (see Table 2) is greater than

TABLE 2. *Comparison of experimental and control
groups*

Index	Difference between groups (Mann-Whitney z)	p	Direction of difference
Mean affect change score for five attitude objects on which the experimental subjects were not manipulated	.07	>.90	—
Affect change score for high-interest attitude object	3.30	<.001	Exp.> control
Cognition change score for high-interest attitude object	2.62	<.01	Exp.> control
Mean change in importance of values associated with the high-interest attitude object	3.15	<.002	Exp.> control
Mean change in instrumentality of high-interest attitude object	3.80	<.0002	Exp.> control

.90. (All probability values reported for this and the following study are two-tailed and, unless otherwise indicated, are obtained through application of the Mann-Whitney Rank Sum Test; Mosteller and Bush, 1954.) The actual change scores upon which the comparison is based are discovered upon inspection to be small enough and enough dispersed in both directions to suggest that they are essentially chance fluctuations. Thus, the two groups do not differ in the characteristic (i.e. test-retest stability of attitudinal affect) of greatest relevance to the testing of the present hypothesis.

The testing of that hypothesis further requires that the experimental manipulation be potent enough to produce sizable alteration in the affective components of the experimental subjects' high-interest attitudes. When the affect change scores for their high-interest, manipulated attitudes are compared to the control subjects' affect change scores for their high-interest, nonmanipulated attitudes, a difference significant at a chance probability of less than .001 is obtained (see Table 2). Inspection of the distributions indicates that this difference is due to the experimental subjects' greater affect change scores, all in the manipulated direction.

Cognitive reorganization in relation to induced affect change. While these findings ensure that certain essential conditions were met, they do not bear upon the major prediction that when affects are altered, *beliefs* about the objects of those affects will be changed in a congruent direction.

The basic test of this prediction involved the computation, from each subject's two performances on the cognitive structure test, of two "indices of cognitive structure" (see pp. 19–20 above) for the high-interest attitude object. The difference between these two indices was computed for each subject, and the difference scores of the experimental subjects were compared to those of the control subjects. On this comparison the experimental subjects show significantly more cognitive change than the control subjects. (Examination shows the cognitive changes achieved by the experimental subjects to be consistent with the affect changes produced by posthypnotic suggestion.) The chance probability of the obtained difference is less than .01 (see Table 2). The median cognition change scores in the experimental and control groups are 167 and 21, respectively. The highest cognition change score in the experimental group is 642; in the control group, 57.

Thus, the major prediction of the present study was confirmed: cognitive reorganization did follow an induced change in affect. Furthermore, this finding lends support to the general homeostatic proposition from which the prediction was derived.

Looking beyond the fact that cognitive reorganization takes place, it may be asked whether such change comes about through modifications of perceived instrumentality, of value importance, or of both. If a person's affect is changed from positive to negative on the issue, say, of Federal medical insurance, will he then see Federal medical insurance as blocking the same values he formerly thought it advanced, or will he renounce the values that led him originally to favor the policy? This question was investigated by computing for each subject an index of *mean change in value importance* and an index of *mean change in perceived instrumentality*. It was first determined which of the 31 values were seen by the subject as instrumentally affected by the high-interest attitude object on at least one of the two administrations of the cognitive structure test. For all these values there were computed the absolute differences between their first and second value importance ratings and their first and second perceived instrumentality ratings. These two groups of differences were used in calculating the subject's separate mean change in value importance and his mean change in perceived instrumentality, respectively.

When the experimental and control groups are compared on these indices it is found (see Table 2) that they differ significantly, the experimental subjects having the higher change scores. Thus, the experimental subjects achieve cognitive reorganization through changes in both the instrumentality and value importance aspects of beliefs about the attitude object. However, since the indices of mean change in value intensity and perceived instrumentality are based upon the computation of absolute differences, it was deemed necessary to examine the experimental subjects' test records to see what *kinds* of underlying change are represented in these indices. Examination reveals that most of the value intensity and perceived instrumentality changes are in directions that contribute to altering the subjects' attitudinal cognitions toward consistency with their altered affects.

The fact that the chance probabilities given in the last two rows of Table 2 are even lower than that for the comparison based on the main index of cognitive structure suggests that some of the changes in value importance and perceived instrumentality are not reflected in changes in the main index. This is found to be due to the fact that some small number of the values for which the typical experimental subject changes either his importance or instrumentality ratings retain zero ratings on the other scale; the product of the multiplication of these two ratings is therefore zero.

Validity of postmanipulation data. Up to this point the assumption has been that the experimental subjects are reflecting "real" (i.e. subjectively experienced) changes in their feelings and beliefs. But it could be argued that their postmanipulation test performances were guided by their notions of how they would behave (or how they would be expected to behave) *if* their affects had changed.

Probably the strongest basis for rejecting this "role-playing" interpretation is simply what the subjects say about their experiences. After the completion of testing but before the force of the posthypnotic suggestion was eliminated (by providing the signal which removed the posthypnotic amnesia), the experimental subjects vigorously defended their affective and cognitive responses against challenges delivered by the tester. When it was pointed out that their present statements were inconsistent with their previous responses the subjects either insisted that they had misunderstood the instructions before the first test administration or else they simply asserted that their previous beliefs were wrong and that their present beliefs were correct. After amnesia removal all the experimental subjects insisted that on the second test their responses had reflected their real feelings and beliefs at the time of testing.

Furthermore, when the experimental subjects are compared to a group of control subjects who went through identical measurement procedures under the instruction to role-play the occurrence of attitude change, a number of striking differences in the patterns of affective and cognitive "change" are obtained. The general significance of these differences is that they support the conclusion that the present hypnotic subjects do experience real change in affect and cognition toward the manipulated attitude object while the role-playing subjects do not.[2] The data from this portion of the present

2. The post-experimental comments of the subjects given instructions to role-play the occurrence of affect change are another source of evidence on this point. Typically they explained, after the completion of testing, that they had been "making believe," "playing the role you gave me," "just having fun with my imagination." That they felt no need to reconcile their test responses with their self-images was revealed in many comments of which the following is an example: "Well, I figured that to be against Negroes that way I would have to be quite a reactionary type—so naturally in all the other questions I changed to the reactionary position. But of course this has nothing to do with what I really feel."

study have been fully described in a previous publication (Rosenberg, 1960).

Process aspects of cognitive reorganization. A fuller understanding of the hypothesized homeostatic aspect of attitude change requires that extensive analysis of the cognitive reorganization process be undertaken. Work in progress at the time of writing is specifically addressed toward this problem; but as a crude beginning it will be useful to summarize a few major impressions based upon the test and interview records of the present experimental subjects.

Four different types of instrumentality change are observed. The most extreme is the simple reversal of instrumentality from positive to negative or negative to positive (e.g. a subject who originally opposes, but after hypnosis favors, the city-manager plan, first sees it as serving, and then as blocking, the negative value "having power and authority over people"). A related form of change is that in which the extremity of an instrumentality rating is reduced without change in its sign (e.g. from, say, $+5$ to $+1$ or $+2$). Another type involves the reduction of an object-value relationship to the absence of any relationship (e.g. a subject who was originally in favor of Federal medical insurance and received a posthypnotic suggestion of negative affect first sees Federal medical insurance as working for the value "people having the right to participate in making decisions which will affect them"; after hypnosis he sees no connection between Federal medical insurance and this value). Still another form of instrumentality change is one in which a value formerly seen as uninfluenced by the attitude object is now seen as being influenced by it.

In addition to instrumentality change, most of the subjects also give evidence of some changes in their evaluation of the value terms. A relatively infrequent form of value change involves the reversal of sign (e.g. a subject who is originally opposed to Negroes moving into white neighborhoods at first gives a negative rating to the value term "people of different backgrounds getting to know each other better"; after hypnosis and receipt of the posthypnotic suggestion of affect reversal the subject judges this to be a positive value. On both occasions he asserts that the value will be served by Negroes moving into white neighborhoods). A more common form of value change is one in which the subject modifies a former belief by reducing the importance of its invoked value without changing its sign.

Analysis of interview material suggests that underlying these various types of cognitive change there are certain basic modes of conceptual reorganization. For example, one of the bases for instrumentality change may best be described by borrowing a phrase from Asch (1940): some subjects seem to change their judgments by *partially* redefining the "object of judgment." Where this occurs, a previously unitary attitude object is broken down into "good" and "bad" component parts; in reorganizing his cognitions the subject then emphasizes one aspect, depending upon whether he has been hypnotically commanded to experience positive or negative feelings toward the object. Similarly, some subjects redefine some of the value terms, thus enabling changes in their importance ratings.

But just as often the attitude objects and value terms seem to hold constant in their meaning. When this is so the locus of cognitive change seems to be in the subjects' thinking about the instrumental relations between objects. At least one aspect of such change is discernible in the available interview material: this might be labeled "the dispositional shift away from value-terminality." What is meant here is simply a tendency to re-examine previously terminal values with regard to their own instrumental implications for other values. For example, in a later experiment, a subject who was against abandoning economic aid to foreign nations was hypnotically commanded to feel favorably toward such a policy. Before hypnosis he had asserted that abandoning economic aid "would handicap the economic development of ex-colonial nations"; after hypnosis he asserted the same belief with the important addition that this effect would be *temporary* and that its long-range results would be to force the ex-colonial nations to become self-reliant and thus more democratic. Some subjects seem to rely heavily upon this kind of "sweet lemon" set, and the comparable "sour grapes" set, as the means for managing large-scale cognitive reorganization in directions consistent with altered affects.

In the main, the forms of concept change and instrumentality change that have been described here seem to depend on the general process of "selective search" that is described in Chapter 4. Some other basic devices underlying cognitive reorganization are suggested by data drawn from the present experiment and from the one described in the next section of this chapter. A more extended and systematic treatment of these devices will be attempted in a later publication.

Restoration of original attitude. A last finding deals with the aftereffects of the experiment upon subjects who had received the hypnotic manipulation of affect. Although no further testing was carried out, the interview records indicate clearly that after the posthypnotic amnesia was removed and the experiment fully explained, all subjects were able once again to establish their original attitudes.[3] The fact that they were able to do this suggests that another issue needs to be examined.

This issue may be delineated by noting that the major proposition upon which this investigation rests is that "when

3. However, in the portion of this experiment concerned with low-interest attitudes (see Rosenberg, 1960) there was evidence (based on interviewing) that at least one subject had retained the altered affect as well as a number of associated new beliefs.

the affective and cognitive components of an attitude are consistent, the attitude is in a stable state"; yet the hypnotic subjects, after having changed their beliefs, seem to revert rapidly to their original attitudinal affects and beliefs once the posthypnotic amnesia has been withdrawn. Thus, can one say that during the experiment a new attitude was established or, merely, that an old attitude was unstabilized? The present experiment does not permit a clear answer to this question. The reinstatement of the pre-experimental attitude may in itself be viewed as the carrying out of a posthypnotic suggestion. A procedure might have been employed in which no suggestion of restoration of the original attitude would have been given; but this would have violated the ethical limits of psychological research.

It would, however, be possible to keep the amnesia for the posthypnotic suggestion intact for a longer period, during which the subject's attitudinal affect and associated cognitions would be retested a number of times. This would make it possible to determine whether attitudes that have undergone reorganization in response to the hypnotic alteration of affect do show some stability over time.

Another question arises from the fact that, except for judgments elicited from the subjects during a final interview, there is no direct evidence as to whether any aspects of the experimentally produced affective or cognitive changes did, in reality, persist. In the experiment reported in the next section certain major procedural innovations suggested by these considerations were employed.

THE DURATION OF COGNITIVE REORGANIZATION

This experiment attempted to sustain the reversed affect for a full week rather than for merely one or two hours. The prediction was that during all of this period the subjects would continue to judge values and their relations to the attitude object in ways consistent with their altered affective responses. It was also predicted that after the removal of the posthypnotic amnesia (and, thus, of the force of the affect manipulation) an over-all restoration of the subject's original cognitive structure would be observed, but that at the same time some aspects of the changes would persist during further testing. The latter prediction was based on the assumption that the arousal and expression of altered cognitions over a long period of time would increase the intensity and certainty with which some of these were held and thus would increase the difficulty of abandoning them when amnesia had been removed.

Method

From a larger group of volunteers, eight new subjects capable of deep hypnosis were recruited and assigned to the experimental group. Eight other subjects untested for hypnotizability but selected so as to match the experimental group in sex, age, and educational level were assigned to a control group.

To enable close comparison of the performances of the separate subjects a criterion had been set that for the issue on which the experimental subjects were to be manipulated, all subjects be as nearly identical as possible in both direction and magnitude of affective response. Earlier investigation had indicated that, of various attitude issues tested, the one that came closest to meeting these specifications in the population from which our subjects were to be drawn was "the proposal that the United States abandon its policy of economic aid to foreign nations." All members of a pilot test group responded at the extreme negative end of an affect scale on this issue.

Accordingly, in an initial individual testing session, each

subject first filled out an affect questionnaire dealing with this and two other issues. As in the previous study, a modified Coombs scale was used which consisted of sixteen positions ranging from extreme positive affect to extreme negative affect.

Following the administration of this instrument each subject was tested with a revised form (employing 32 value items) of the cognitive structure device used in the previous studies. On this test, which was administered by a person other than the hypnotist, the subject gave his value importance judgments for each of the items, and then in three separate administrations of the instrumentality portion of the test he separately judged each of the three attitude objects respectively for their value-attaining and value-blocking powers.

All of these procedures were repeated in five further testing sessions. Thus at the end of the experiment there were available two kinds of control data: those obtained from the control subjects who underwent no hypnotic affect manipulation and those obtained from the experimental subjects with reference to the two attitude objects for which they received no hypnotic affect manipulation.

Three days after the initial testing session each experimental subject while in hypnosis was given the following post-hypnotic suggestion:

> After you awake, and continuing until our next meeting, you will feel very strongly opposed to the United States policy of giving economic aid to foreign nations. The mere idea of the United States giving economic aid to foreign nations will make you feel very displeased and disgusted. Until your next meeting with me you will continue to feel very strong and thorough opposition to the United States policy of economic aid to foreign nations.

> You will have no memory whatsoever of this sugges-
> tion having been made . . . until the amnesia is re-
> moved by my giving you the signal at our next session.
> The signal will be that I will write the word *geology* on
> a piece of paper and then hand the paper to you. Only
> when I do that at our meeting next week will the am-
> nesia be removed.

It should be noted that while the affect measure was phrased
in terms of the proposal that the policy of economic aid be
abandoned, the hypnotic manipulation is addressed to the
subject's affect toward the policy of economic aid as such.
This procedure was intended to demonstrate that the subject does not respond only to the specific verbal formula used
in the hypnotic instruction, but that he interiorizes the hypnotic command in a meaningful and generalized way. Thus,
if commanded to feel negatively toward the policy of economic aid, he should express positive affect toward the proposal that the policy be abandoned.

After awakening from hypnosis the subject was turned over
to the tester and was remeasured, on all three attitude areas,
on affect and cognition respectively. Two days later, and
again two days after that, these tests were administered again.
Three days after the fourth testing session (e.g. exactly one
week after the delivery of the posthypnotic suggestion of
affect reversal) the subject again met with the hypnotist. In
this session the amnesia for the contents of the hypnotic
session was removed and the experiment was then explained
to the subject. The explanation described in detail the
prediction that affect change would lead to cognitive change
and also included an examination of the subject's test records. Three days after the amnesia removal, and then after
seven more days had passed, additional sessions were held
in each of which all testing procedures were repeated. As in

the previous experiment, it was possible to prevent the hypnotic subjects from suspecting the connection between the testing and the hypnotic session until the time when amnesia was removed and the purpose of the experiment was explained. However, toward the end of the first week, two subjects did gradually develop vague and uncertain suspicions that some sort of hypnotic manipulation might have been used. But both insisted that they had no *memory* for any such event; they were merely "reasoning" from the fact that they had undergone sudden and intense changes in their feelings and beliefs on the foreign aid issue.

Identical procedures were used with the control and the experimental subjects, except that the former had no contact with the hypnotist and underwent no affect manipulation. A further innovation was that all the subjects were required to "think out loud" during the cognitive structure testing. Thus, while sorting the value cards for their "importance" they were directed to tell "what the card means to you." While sorting the values for the influence upon them of a specific attitude object they were to explicate upon the nature of the instrumental relationship. All comments were recorded on tape.

Results

The comparability of the experimental and control groups. As in the previous study, it was necessary to establish that affect changes shown by the hypnotic subjects were due to the manipulation rather than to a general characteristic of affective instability. Since each subject took the same tests on six different occasions, it was possible to study stability of affective response toward the nonmanipulated attitude objects over a greater time period. Following a procedure used in the previous study, when the experimental subjects' and the control subjects' mean affect change scores based upon the two nonmanipulated attitude areas are compared, it is found that the former show no more instability than the latter. Table 3 reports the findings of the comparisons based upon the change scores from the second, third, fourth, fifth, and sixth testing sessions, respectively.

TABLE 3. *Experimental and control subjects compared on their mean change scores for the two nonmanipulated attitude objects*

Tests from which mean change scores are computed	MEAN AFFECT CHANGE		MEAN COGNITION CHANGE	
	Mann-Whitney z	p	Mann-Whitney z	p
Test 1—Test 2	.89	>.35	.25	>.75
Test 1—Test 3	.10	>.90	.46	>.60
Test 1—Test 4	.46	>.60	.57	>.55
Test 1—Test 5	.05	>.95	.57	>.55
Test 1—Test 6	.17	>.80	.17	>.80

Exactly equivalent findings are obtained when the comparisons are repeated for the mean cognition change scores of the same subjects (see Table 3). Thus, although differing in hypnotizability, the two groups of subjects do not differ in the stability over time of their affective and cognitive responses associated with attitude objects that have not been manipulated.

It was necessary also to determine whether the affect manipulation was potent enough to produce sizable alterations (lasting until amnesia removal) in the feelings of the experimental subjects. When the two groups are compared for their affect change scores on the foreign aid issue it is found that in all three possible comparisons (the differences between the original affect score and the affect scores from the second, third, and fourth test administrations respectively) [4] all the

4. The two groups of subjects are not properly comparable with regard to change scores based upon the fifth and sixth administrations, respectively,

change scores for the experimental subjects exceed the change scores for the control subjects.[5] Thus in each case the difference between the groups is significant at a probability of less than .002 (see Table 4). Similar findings are obtained when the experimental subjects' affect change scores on the foreign aid issue are compared to the means of their affect change scores on the two nonmanipulated issues (see Table 5).

TABLE 4. *Experimental and control subjects compared on their change scores for the attitude object ("foreign aid") on which the experimental subjects were manipulated*

Tests from which change scores are computed	AFFECT CHANGE Mann-Whitney z	p	COGNITION CHANGE Mann-Whitney z	p
Test 1—Test 2	3.30	<.002	2.36	<.02
Test 1—Test 3	3.30	<.002	1.99	<.05
Test 1—Test 4	3.30	<.002	2.05	<.05

Cognitive reorganization in relation to induced affect change. As in the previous study, the major question was whether with the alteration of an attitudinal affect there occurs a corresponding and consistent reorganization of beliefs. In the present study, however, it is possible to ask this question not only about cognitive changes occurring immediately after the achievement of affect reversal but also with regard to the cognitions asserted by the subjects two days after, and again four days after, the hypnotic manipulation.

of the measures referring to the foreign aid issue. This is because before the fifth session, in undergoing amnesia removal, the experimental subjects came to see the special experimental significance of the foreign aid issue and had its relation to the experimental hypothesis explained to them; the control subjects, on the other hand, remained unenlightened.

5. In no case does an experimental subject show a change of less than 13 scale points out of a possible 15; most of the control subjects, on the other hand, have affect change scores of zero.

If it were found that during the third and fourth testing sessions the cognitive changes achieved immediately after affect reversal tended to disappear or weaken, then this would suggest that the effect is confined to the "afterglow" of hypnotic manipulation. If, on the other hand, it were found that such changes persisted for as long as the reversed affect persists, additional evidence would be supplied for the main prediction and for the proposition that when the affective and cognitive components of an attitude are consistent with one another then that attitude is in a stable state.

Two kinds of evidence are available on this question. One involves comparing the experimental subjects' cognition change scores to those of the control subjects, just as was done in the previous study. Thus when for each subject we compute the amount of change, from the first to the second test, in his beliefs about economic aid to foreign nations, the experimental subjects show significantly more of such change than do the control subjects ($p < .02$, see Table 4). The median change scores in the experimental and control groups lie between 210 and 195, and 64 and 57, respectively. These findings, since they are based upon cognitive changes observed in the first test performance after hypnosis, serve as a direct replication of the major finding in the previous study. When an identical analysis is carried out with reference to cognitive changes based on the third test administration, a difference of the same sort is obtained ($p < .05$, see Table 4). The median change score for the experimental group lies between 161 and 125 and for the control group between 36 and 26. For the analysis based upon the fourth administration of the cognitive structure test the obtained difference has a probability of less than .05 (see Table 4) and the median change scores for the experimental and control groups lie between 183 and 167, and 87 and 70, respectively. In general then, this evidence indicates that over a period of five days during which the hypnotically altered affects of the experimental subjects persisted, there was also a comparable persistence of the patterns of cognitive alteration consistent with those altered affects.

The second kind of evidence against which the major prediction may be tested involves using the experimental subjects as their own controls and comparing each subject's cognition change score on the manipulated issue to the mean of his cognition change scores for the two nonmanipulated issues. When such a comparison is carried out with change

TABLE 5. *Probabilities of the differences between the change scores for the manipulated and nonmanipulated attitudes* *

Tests from which change scores are computed	Affect change	Cognition change
Test 1—Test 2	.008	.024
Test 1—Test 3	.008	.024
Test 1—Test 4	.008	.008
Test 1—Test 5	Not sig.	.056
Test 1—Test 6	Not sig.	.064

* The probabilities are obtained through application of the Randomization Test for Matched Pairs (Siegal, 1956). All significant differences are in the direction: manipulated attitude > mean of nonmanipulated attitudes.

scores computed from the second testing session (the session conducted immediately after the hypnotic manipulation) application of the Randomization Test for Matched Pairs (Siegal, 1956) indicates that the pattern of greater cognitive change toward the manipulated object exceeds chance expectation at a probability of .024 (see Table 5). Illustrative of the data from which this finding is obtained is the fact that when the eight experimental subjects are ranked on the size of the difference between the two change scores the largest obtained difference is 343, while the median lies between 200 and 208.

When an identical analysis is carried out with change scores based upon the differences between the subject's cognitive responses on the prehypnotic test administration and his responses on the third and fourth test administrations respectively, differences of equal strength are obtained. As Table 5 indicates, when change scores are calculated between the first and third test administrations the difference between extent of cognitive change toward the manipulated issue and the two nonmanipulated issues is significant at a chance probability of .024. When computed from the fourth test administration the difference between the two change scores has a chance probability of .008. In the former case the greatest obtained difference between change scores is 311, with the median between 116 and 184; in the latter case the greatest obtained difference between change scores is 359, and the median lies between 137 and 149.

It should not be concluded, however, that *all* the beliefs expressed by the typical subject are consistent with the altered attitudinal affect. Usually some of his original beliefs persist within the new structure and are inconsistent with its overall import, though typically the intensity with which these beliefs are held is reduced after the affect manipulation. But, as was noted above, it is not assumed that total and perfect consistency need obtain in a stable attitude structure; all that is assumed is that affective-cognitive inconsistency, if present at all, is at a level below the individual's tolerance limit. At any rate, examination of the postmanipulation attitude structures of the present subjects reveals, in most cases, a sizable amount of cognitive reorganization in the direction consistent with the altered affect.

As in the previous study, one might ask whether the cognitive reorganizations were achieved by changes in the perceived instrumentality of the attitude object or in the "importance" of the values affected or both. Comparing the experimental and control groups on the same mean change indices used in the previous study, it was found that, unlike the results obtained in that study, they do not differ significantly from each other. However this index is based upon absolute changes and disregards their direction (i.e. in the present experiment its application disregards the question of whether the changes are supportive of, or inconsistent with, the anti-foreign aid affect). Further analysis of the test records reveals that, while the members of the two groups do show equal degrees of *absolute* change in their judgments of value intensity and perceived instrumentality, the *directions* of the changes are quite different. This analysis involved computing for each person the amount of absolute change between the intensity-instrumentality product for each value that was not judged as unaffected by foreign aid (i.e. zero instrumentality) on both of the cognitive tests used in the comparison. The absolute sum of all such product changes was computed. It was then determined what portion of that sum represented changes in the direction consistent with the affect manipulation. A ratio was computed for each subject representing the proportion of his total amount of change that was consistent with opposition to foreign aid.

When the two groups are compared on the ratio based upon the first and second administrations of the cognitive structure test, application of the Rank Sum Test yields a probability of less than .004. In an identical comparison based on the first and third test administrations the obtained probability is less than .05; in the comparison based on the first and fourth test administrations the obtained probability is less than .01. In each of these three comparisons the significant findings come from the fact that the product changes of the hypnotic subjects were largely in the anti-foreign aid direction while those of the control subjects were smaller and were randomly dispersed in both directions.

The fact that the present control subjects showed less test-retest reliability in their cognitive responses than did the control subjects in the first study is interpreted as due to the fact that for the former group a number of days intervened between each test administration while for the latter the time between the two tests was one hour or less.

Restoration of original attitude. When, three days after amnesia removal, the experimental subjects went through their fifth testing sessions, all of them expressed negative affect toward the proposal that foreign aid be abandoned. Four returned to their original "extreme negative" affect position toward abandoning foreign aid; two others fell one scale point short of their original positions, and the remaining two were three scale points short of their original positions. Compared against the control data based on the two unmanipulated attitudes the subjects show no significant difference (see Table 5) between their original affective responses and their affective responses after amnesia removal.

In the previous experiment no test data were collected after the experimental subjects' amnesias were removed. In most cases, however, interviewing indicated that, on the whole, the subjects' original attitudes had been re-established. It was pointed out, though, that the hypnotic instruction stated that after remembering the posthypnotic suggestion the subject's attitude would return to "normal." Similarly, in the present study, each experimental subject was told: *"Until your next meeting with me* you will continue to feel very strong and thorough opposition to the United States policy of economic aid to foreign nations." Yet it might be expected that after elaborating and rationalizing his new affect during three separate administrations of the cognitive structure test the subject would have become aware of, and identified with, a number of new arguments in support of his altered cognitions. Thus it was predicted that, even after removal of amnesia and restoration of the original affective response, some aspects of the posthypnotic cognitive reorganization would be found to persist.

To check this possibility there was computed for each experimental subject his cognition change scores based upon the first and fifth and first and sixth test administrations, respectively. When the first group of change scores is examined it is found that for all but one of the subjects the cognition change score referring to the abandonment of foreign aid is larger than the mean of the cognition change scores for the two unmanipulated issues (p = .056, see Table 5). The magnitudes of the differences upon which this finding is based are noticeably lower than those from the last cognitive testing before amnesia removal: the highest obtained difference between the two cognition change scores before amnesia removal was 359, and the median of the difference scores was located between 137 and 149; after amnesia removal the highest obtained difference is 211, and the median lies between 99 and 103. It should be added that in all but one case the actual indices of cognitive structure achieved on the fifth test administration are negative numbers (i.e. the over-all balance of the cognitions is consistent with the restored negative affect toward abandoning the policy of economic aid to foreign nations.)

Thus tests given three days after amnesia removal show that the experimental subjects have reorganized many of their beliefs in the direction of their original affective responses; but they have not yet formed cognitive structures as extreme in their support of the foreign aid policy as those with which they started. Furthermore, even though ten days after the removal of amnesia they have come still closer to restoration of their original beliefs, they still hold to patterns of cognition that, while consistent with their original affects, are less extreme than those with which they entered the experiment (see Table 5).

The test records reveal that these changes are due to two different forms of variation from the original cognitive structures. After amnesia removal the typical subject manages to reassert most of his original beliefs but frequently at lower levels of certainty ("perceived instrumentality") about the asserted relationships. At the same time some subjects retain intact a few cognitive assertions that were consistent with the altered affect and are inconsistent with the restored affect.

This last finding might be interpreted as reducing the generality of the proposition concerning affective-cognitive consistency in attitudes. But it should be remembered that at the time of the first testing after amnesia removal, all but one of the subjects had managed to restore their cognitive structures to general consistency with the re-established affects. If they continue to avow a few anti-foreign aid beliefs and to assert pro-foreign aid beliefs with somewhat less certainty than on the premanipulation cognitive test, it is worth noting that during the major portion of the experiment they have been examining the other side; new considerations about means-end relationships discovered while adapting to the affect reversal may persist merely by virtue of their apparent merit to the subject or because the subject needs to maintain an image of himself as a person whose thinking on social issues has some stability and is not completely geared to experimental manipulations.[6]

6. However, it is not suggested that the cognitive responses obtained during the last test administration represent the subjects' final and fixed views of the issue. To the contrary, it was expected that with termination of the testing sessions and with the further passage of time still further restoration of the subjects' original attitudinal cognitions would occur. This would be due to frequent and continuing exposure to the kinds of communications (issuing from others and from the subject himself) that had contributed to the establishment of their original pro-foreign aid attitudes. Interviewing

At any rate, it has already been noted that the proposition
that affective-cognitive consistency is a basic characteristic of
attitudes does not preclude the possibility of tolerance for
some degree of partial (and, in this case, probably temporary)
inconsistency *within* a cognitive structure. This would be
particularly relevant when, in their over-all direction, the
attitudinal cognitions are consistent with the person's affective set toward the object around which they are organized.

One last point worth noting is that with those subjects
whose final cognitive structures show the greatest change there
is some evidence, based both upon analysis of their "think out
loud" protocols and upon the results of post-experimental
interviewing, that the object of judgment has undergone some
lasting redefinition. An example is one subject who, after
receiving the posthypnotic suggestion, redefined economic
aid into two major components, financial and technological,
and then elaborated a set of beliefs about the undesirable
consequences of financial aid. After amnesia removal he once
again saw economic aid to foreign nations as compounded
of both specific types of aid but tended to lay greater stress
than he had originally on the technological aspect. Of his
few persisting anti-foreign aid beliefs he said spontaneously
that they "would be true only if [they] refer to just giving
money and not giving technical assistance."

IMPLICATIONS

In an earlier section of this chapter there was presented a
general proposition that the production of gross inconsistency
between the affective and cognitive components of an attitude
renders that attitude unstable. From this proposition two
hypotheses were drawn. Some studies by other investigators

---

conducted about one month later with six of the subjects yielded clear, if
impressionistic, evidence in support of this expectation; each of these subjects seemed to have achieved still greater consistency between his restored
positive affect toward foreign aid and his cognitions about it.

were interpreted as confirming the first of these, i.e. that sizable alteration of attitudinal cognitions would generate consistent change in the affective response toward the attitude object. The second hypothesis was that the direct alteration of the affective component of a social attitude would, if it were so strongly established as to be "irreversible," eventuate in cognitive reorganization consistent with such alteration. Taking the data that have been presented as confirming this hypothesis, we may conclude that additional support has been provided for the general proposition from which it was derived. The present studies and the afore-mentioned ones by Carlson (1956), Cartwright (1949), Peak (1959), Smith (1949), Woodruff (1942) and Woodruff and Di Vesta (1948) suggest also that this theoretical approach may be extended through further analysis of the two sequences of attitude change that have been hypothesized. It seems possible, too, that these two sequences may serve as a model for the situation in which attitudes are originally acquired as well as the situation in which they undergo change.

A two-sequence model of attitude dynamics

It is proposed then that all types of attitude acquisition and attitude change may be understood as the result of the person's having undergone one (or a blend) of two discriminably distinct sequences. It is not contended that attitude change is an inevitable result of the arousal of affective-cognitive inconsistency; but rather that, when attitudes *do* change, they change through the operation of either one or both of these sequences.

The sequence originating in modification of cognitive response. Either through direct encounter with an object or with communications about that object a person acquires one or more beliefs, each of which links the object to some "locus of affect" (i.e. some other "object," state, or condition with which a stable positive or negative affective response is regularly associated).[7] In proportion to the strength, number, and mutual consistency of these new beliefs there will be generated a similar, but tentative, affective disposition toward the object in question. When the object formerly elicited no stable affective response and was not believed to be related to any affect locus (i.e. when no previous attitude existed) the newly generated affective disposition will become stabilized as the person's attitudinal affect toward that object. When a previous and opposite attitude *did* exist, and when the new beliefs replace the old ones or predominate over them, then the discrepancy between these new beliefs and the original affective disposition will be resolved by that disposition giving way (at least to a degree that reduces overall affective-cognitive inconsistency to a magnitude below the intolerance threshold for the attitude) to the newly generated and opposite affective disposition.

The sequence originating in modification of affective response. Either through reinforcement in association with an object or through reinforcement for the imitative or trial-and-error "rehearsal" of an affective response to an object, a person acquires an affective disposition toward it.[8] The strength of this disposition varies with the intensity, timing, frequency, and consistency of the reinforcement received. In

7. It might be useful to regard arbitrarily such affect loci as *attitude objects* only when the affects associated with them are associated not by virtue of the object's consummatory, goallike character but rather because the object is believed to provide access to positive or negative goal states. When such affect loci arouse affect by virtue of their consummatory, goallike character they may be classed as "values." It will be recognized that such a distinction is implicit in the experimental studies reported in this chapter.

8. Such reinforcement need not come only from external agencies; affect expression may in itself provide need reduction and conflict resolution, and these may operate to reinforce the expressed affect. In this respect much of the present analysis may be tied to the kind of psychodynamic approach to attitudes exemplified in the contributions of Adorno, Frenkel-Brunswik, et al. (1950), Smith, Bruner, and White (1956), and Sarnoff, Katz, and Mc-Clintock (1954).

proportion to the strength of the affective disposition the person will tentatively adopt and/or invent beliefs that are consistent with it and that relate its object to other affect loci. When no previous attitude existed these beliefs will become stabilized as the person's attitudinal cognitions. When a previous and opposite attitude *did* exist, and when the new affective disposition replaces or predominates over the old one, then the discrepancy between this new disposition and the original beliefs will be resolved by those beliefs giving way (at least to a degree that reduces over-all affective-cognitive inconsistency to a magnitude below the individual's intolerance threshold for the attitude) to the new and opposite beliefs.

These two sequences are assumed to operate (1) only when the degree of affective-cognitive inconsistency exceeds the individual's present tolerance for such inconsistency; (2) only when consistency is sought by the person (see the discussion below of other modes of response to affective-cognitive inconsistency); and (3) only when the original alteration of either the affective or cognitive component has been sufficiently compelling, and is strongly enough maintained, to be irreversible. Where the last-mentioned condition is not met, it may be assumed that the least effortful response to the experience of an intolerable degree of affective-cognitive inconsistency is to undo the original inconsistency-establishing change, e.g. to reject the change-inducing communication. Thus whether attitude change or attitude restoration results when conditions (1) and (2) are met will depend on a number of additional factors. One of these would be the sheer potency of the original communication in comparison to the original strength of the attitude component(s) against which it is directed. In the present experiment a hypnotic command of affect reversal must be assumed to have been a highly potent communication. But apart from communication potency, other factors must be assumed to play prominent roles in the establishment of irreversible inconsistency. Among these might be order-of-presentation variables (Hovland et al., 1957) and aspects of the personality of the subject (Janis et al., 1959).

Conditions under which consistency is sought

It should be clear that the foregoing is a formulation of two "ideal types" and that in real life both processes may be in operation at the same time or in alternation. The formulation makes no attempt to list all the person and situation variables that might be operative in the posited processes. One such variable, which has already been mentioned, that must be assumed to have great relevance to the operation of the two sequences may be conceived as an intolerance for affective-cognitive inconsistency. It is assumed that such intolerance characterizes persons generally; but it has already been acknowledged that persons (and their specific attitudes) seem to vary in the degree of inconsistency which must be encountered (i.e. the threshold which must be surpassed) before intolerance is experienced. At the same time it cannot be assumed that intolerance when aroused necessarily sets a person to strive for the restoration of true affective-cognitive consistency.

Indeed, in the face of considerable everyday evidence to the contrary, it cannot be argued that any individual always handles the experience of affective-cognitive inconsistency in only one way, e.g. by striving toward final consistency. It was stated above that measures of "repression or deverbalization may be brought into play in dealing with inconsistencies that, . . . by virtue of the strength of the forces or facts that maintain them . . . do not admit of reduction or resolution." Expanding further upon this point, it is suggested that such devices serve the goal of inconsistency avoidance through "fragmentation" of the attitude structure; i.e. through effectively isolating the affective from the related but inconsistent cognitive component by rendering either one or both of these unavailable for direct, articulated perusal.[9] Thus the present theory's underlying proposition is not that affective-cognitive inconsistency in an attitude structure will always be followed by restoration of consistency, but rather that, if it exceeds the individual's tolerance threshold, it will always produce "activity" which will continue until the awareness of inconsistency—the tension elicited by it—is effectively reduced.

Nevertheless, it was contended that the restoration of consistency is the outcome most commonly achieved when persons are enmeshed in affective-cognitive inconsistency with regard to objects of social attitudes. Implied here is the point that when a pattern of affective-cognitive inconsistency is bound up with, or derives from, continuing personality conflicts, there is less likelihood of integrative reorganization. Most social attitudes that have been rendered inconsistent are not so bound up, and typically the individual is potentially capable of restoring them toward balance; whether he will actually undertake to do so will depend on whether his "intolerance-for-inconsistency" threshold for that attitude has been surpassed.[10]

9. A closely related but much less effective way of attempting to avoid an intolerable inconsistency that cannot be resolved is simply to try to ignore it by directing one's attention to other matters. It is hypothesized that the likelihood of further encounter with the object or issue to which the inconsistency refers (or with communications about it) will usually render this a temporary and unstable expedient; if the inconsistency remains incapable of resolution this comparatively ineffective strategy of avoidance will be likely in time to give way to fragmentation-producing measures. However, the alternative possibility of continuing to vacillate between confrontation and avoidance of an irreducible inconsistency must also be noted (see Chapter 4).

10. The possibility that individuals may sometimes accept sizable inconsistencies and maintain them in active awareness must be taken into account in the construction of theories of response consistency. In the present limited formulation this issue is dealt with through the concept of the intolerance-for-

An important question suggested by the foregoing analysis is whether, apart from individual variations in strength of the tendency to seek and defend affective-cognitive consistency, there may be other factors to which this threshold is related. In general terms it is hypothesized that the intolerance threshold value of some specific attitude of a particular person at a particular time is influenced not only by aspects of his personality but also by aspects of the structure and content of the attitude and by aspects of his present situation. For example, experiences reported by those who conduct attitude interviews or, for that matter, by careful observers of normal argumentative discourse, suggest that when affective-cognitive inconsistency is established in a context which forces the person to think closely about it, then the intolerance for inconsistency is maximized. Particularly is this true when the person believes that the product of his thought will be available to others who will judge him by that product. Whether striving toward restoration of consistency is more a function of such situational factors or of a deeply internalized ego ideal or of certain structural and content aspects of the inconsistent attitude, or is equally a function of all of these, is beyond the scope of the present formulation. All that need be asserted here is that attitudinal affective-cognitive inconsistency is an unstable state and that when it is not handled by rejection of the inconsistency-arousing communications, or by some process that culminates in fragmentation of the attitude structure or by similar means, then it is handled by changing the affective or the cognitive component of the attitude. It is in this case (assumed to be common for social attitudes), and in this case only, that the two

---

inconsistency threshold: thus any possible instance of true affective-cognitive inconsistency that does not mobilize activity leading to its avoidance or reduction is, by virtue of that concept, regarded as possessing infrathreshold intensity.

attitude change sequences detailed above are assumed to be operative.

Evaluation of contrary evidence

The assumption that affective-cognitive inconsistency in social attitudes is usually handled by changing the components of the attitude to restore it to consistency would not be accepted by all students of attitude processes. As contrary evidence, it might be pointed out that experimental subjects and survey respondents are sometimes found to hold stable social attitudes that are impressively lacking in consistency. From the present point of view one possible interpretation would be that in many such cases the inconsistency is not of sufficient magnitude to disturb the person. But often one of a number of other interpretations may be applicable.

One possibility is that a subject may, at the time of testing, be working through and reorganizing an inconsistent attitude structure. Whether the communications or experiences that rendered the structure inconsistent were encountered before testing or whether they are part of the test setting, it would be expected that if retested later such inconsistency would have been reduced.

Probably more common are those "inconsistencies" that are more apparent than real. The false appearance of extensive affective-cognitive inconsistency in a social attitude is frequently due to deficient methodology or to the misuse of attitude measuring devices. Thus, frequently subjects who have no stable affective set toward a specific object will nevertheless respond to an affect scale by choosing some non-neutral position. Such invalid test responses may be guided by unreliable reference to related objects or by calculating the expectations of the tester; but as pseudo-affective responses they will necessarily lack an associated body of clearly consistent cognitions. When such a subject is interviewed or tested for associated cognitions he will tend to draw them from other attitude structures in which they do fit together with associated affects, or he may improvise responses as invalid as those he gave on the affect measure.

Yet it is not unknown for a subject who seems to hold a real and stable affect toward an object to report many beliefs which are inconsistent with that affect. In the author's opinion this is usually a consequence of the use of some cognitive testing device which does not allow the subject to deal with the goals and values that for him are salient *relata* of the attitude object. When test devices are used to map cognitive aspects of attitudes they must provide the subject with a range of reference concepts wide enough to include those to which, as the subject sees it, the attitude object is truly related.

A further explanation for spurious evidence of inconsistency is the fact that subjects are not always willing or able to report their beliefs. A suspicion that the interviewer holds contrary beliefs, or an awareness that his private beliefs violate normative standards, may limit the subject's expression. Still other forces making for difficulty in, or apathy toward, communication of attitudinal cognitions might be imagined.

Despite these considerations it would seem that most persons are aware of having at least a few intense and stable affective responses for which they cannot offer any impressive cognitive support. Many such cases exemplify a point that has already been made: when affective-cognitive inconsistencies either derive from or express continuing personality-based conflicts, mechanisms of deverbalization, inattention, and isolation (or broadly speaking, repressive devices) are commonly employed which serve the goal of inconsistency avoidance by effectively isolating the affective component; this can happen through "repression" of the cognitive component. Such de-integration is well known in clinical experience. There is, however, some inconclusive evidence that still other types of intense but "cognitionless" affect occur in which the unavailable cognitive material is not contradictory to the affective pattern but in fact consistent with it. Thus both clinical and experimental data suggest that various forms of insightless anxiety (as found in the classic phobias) and similarly certain intense positive and negative affects toward persons, though seemingly cognitionless, are in fact embedded in structures composed of unconscious beliefs (or better, percepts) about the relations of these objects with other affect loci. Such a pattern of unconscious percepts may become associated with a particular affect through either or both of the two attitude-generating sequences posited above. The inability to verbalize such percepts may come from the fact that they were acquired pre-verbally; or it may be due to their being derived and developed through symbol-substitution processes for which there is no available consensual vocabulary; or such beliefs may involve various kinds of magical-irrational relationships of the sort that individuals are trained to disavow as they acquire the ego habits of conformity to consensual reality. Confirming this extended conjecture is the fact that through free association, hypnotic exploration, and dream investigation ostensibly cognitionless affects are frequently found to be rich in associated cognitive material.

Mediational aspects of inconsistency reduction. Little has been said so far about the mediating aspects of the process in which affective-cognitive inconsistencies are reduced or eliminated. One way of generating hypotheses about these mediational aspects is to examine the kind of cognitive reorganization demonstrated in the present studies in the light of a related theoretical approach reported by Rosenberg and Abelson in Chapter 4 of this volume. This approach, in distinction to the present one which has been developed to apply to the problems of attitude dynamics, is intended to deal with inconsistency reduction more generally and in more molecular terms. The kind of affective-cognitive constellation that has here been called an attitude structure may be represented as a group of (object-relation-object) cognitive units or "bands" which are identical with regard to one of their component concepts (an affectively significant attitude object) and different from each other with regard to the other component concept (in this study the "values"). All objects involved in such bands may be designated as affect loci; i.e. their psychological presence arouses stable affective reaction in the person. In the present experiment the relationships between affect loci have been limited to relationships of positive and negative instrumentality, but many other types of relationships are conceivable (see Abelson and Rosenberg, 1958).

A number of recent models (Abelson and Rosenberg, 1958; Cartwright and Harary, 1956; Heider, 1946, 1958; Newcomb, 1953; Osgood and Tannenbaum, 1955) have drawn the distinction between balanced and unbalanced bands (cognitions, beliefs, perceptions, assertions, etc.): a *balanced* band is one in which two affectively positive objects are seen as positively related, two affectively negative objects are seen as positively related, or an affectively positive and an affectively negative object are seen as negatively related; an *unbalanced* cognitive band is one in which a negative relation exists between two affectively negative objects or between two affectively positive objects, or a positive relation exists between an affectively positive object and an affectively negative object.

From this point of view it is meaningful to characterize stable attitudes as structures in which all or most of the bands are balanced. In terms of the present study, if the attitudinal affect is positive, most of the related beliefs will be ones which assert a positive relation between the attitude object and some other locus of positive affect, or else they will be ones which assert a negative relation between the attitude object and some other locus of negative affect. If the attitudinal affect is negative most of the related beliefs will be ones which assert a positive relation between the attitude object and some other locus of negative affect, or else they will be ones which assert a negative relation between the attitude object and some locus of positive affect. It may be postulated that unbalanced bands are, in comparison to balanced bands, *unstable;* that persons holding them are driven to so transform them as to restore them to balance.

In the light of these considerations our conceptualization of the phenomenon demonstrated by the present experiment may be extended to account for some aspects of the process that occurs between the affect manipulation and the achievement of cognitive reorganization. By changing the affective sign associated with the attitude object, the hypnotic manipulation creates, in a single change, states of imbalance in all of those cognitive units which were previously balanced (and, at the same time, it creates balance in those few units, if any, which were previously unbalanced). The assumed consequence is that the person now becomes motivated to restore these newly unbalanced bands to balance.

Pursuing the implications of this approach it can be shown that any band can be restored to balance through changing either one of its signs or all three of them. Clearly, changing only one sign will be a less effortful method of balance restoration than changing all three.

In effect the person who has undergone a change in the affective sign of an attitude object and, as a consequence, is now in the unstable state in which imbalance characterizes all or most of the belief bands in which that object figures has available to him three kinds of single-sign changes by which each of the unbalanced bands may be separately restored to balance. One solution would be to change the sign of the *attitude object* and thus restore all the unbalanced bands to balance. In the present experiment this would mean rejecting the hypnotic command of affect reversal. But if the reinforcing environment that surrounds the person is so arranged that he cannot reject the affect-changing influence (whether it originates in hypnotic instruction, strong group norms, parental demands, the need to resolve an inner conflict, etc.), only two other kinds of change are available for returning any given unbalanced band to a state of balance: the person can either change the sign of the *relationship* between the two objects involved or he can change the sign of the *remaining object*.

In the terms of the present experiment, the first of these alternatives involves changing a perception of positive instrumentality to negative and vice versa or, for that matter, denying the existence of any relationship (a judgment of "zero" instrumentality). A milder form of this alternative is to reduce the extremity of an instrumentality rating without changing its sign. The second alternative is represented in this experiment by changing the sign of, or significantly reducing the magnitude of, the value involved in a particular object-relation-object band. On the basis of one further consideration it becomes clear that the first of the two possible changes is typically the less psychologically costly of the two: while a balancing change in the perceived relation between two objects will not usually tend to unbalance some other object-relation-object band, a balancing change in the affective evaluation of the second object will frequently unbalance some object-relation-object unit belonging to another attitude structure. Thus if a subject has undergone change from negative to positive in his affect toward Federal medical insurance and is faced with his earlier assertion that Federal medical insurance will lead to "socialism," if he now decides that socialism is good, other formerly balanced object-relation-object assertions will now become unbalanced; i.e. "the closed shop (which I dislike) leads to socialism (which I dislike)" now becomes "the closed shop (which I dislike) leads to socialism (which I like)" or "socialism (which I dislike) is a consequence of atheism (which I dislike)" now becomes "socialism (which I like) is a consequence of atheism (which I dislike)." However, changing the asserted relation between the two objects (e.g. "Federal medical insurance *combats and prevents* socialism") enables reduction of imbalance on one band without creating imbalance on other bands.

These considerations help to account for an incidental finding, not previously discussed, that the hypnotic subjects tend to rely upon instrumentality change significantly more than upon value change in reorganizing their cognitive structures to accommodate to the imposed reversals of attitudinal affects. It is consistent too with a finding reported elsewhere (Rosenberg, 1960) that subjects who role-play the occurrence of affect change show significantly more change than hypnotic subjects in the intensities of values involved in their attitudinal cognitions.

A large question that still remains to be dealt with is how sign changes come about: how the person manages to alter his over-all evaluation of an object or of its relation to another object. While some impressionistic answers were offered in connection with the first affect change study, the data from the second study will enable a more precise investigation of this question. Further analysis of the "think out loud" protocols will make it possible to test some of the hypotheses about underlying microprocesses that are stated in Chapter 4. (For example in the relatively rare case in which the sign, rather than merely the intensity, of a value undergoes change it may be asked whether the possible creation of consequent imbalance on other bands involving that value is circumvented by the use of one of the mechanisms described on pp. 154–156.)

Among other questions that seem to require further investigation are the following: Are beliefs involving abstractly defined objects more subject to instrumentality (or, more generally, relational) change than those that involve more concretely defined objects? Does change of sign of an object require at least implicit redefinition or can it occur under conditions of true and total object constancy?

CHAPTER 3

A Syllogistic Analysis of
Cognitive Relationships

WILLIAM J. MCGUIRE

THE "RATIONAL MAN" CONCEPT, long out of fashion in the behavioral sciences, is now undergoing a remarkable revival in the study of cognition. More and more, theory and research are being based on the postulate that a person's need to maintain harmony between his feelings, thoughts, and actions is a powerful determinant of his belief systems and of his gross behavior.

There have been a number of approaches to this modern version of the "rational man" concept. The earliest was probably Sumner's (1907) "strain of consistency," although present-day theories owe more to Heider's "tendency toward balance" (1946); the most complete statement of his position is to be found in his recent book (1958). Heider's line of descent may be separately traced to both Cartwright and Harary's "balanced structures" (1956) and to Abelson and Rosenberg's "balanced matrices" (1958). Closely allied to these notions is Newcomb's "stress toward symmetry" (1953). While the "tendency toward increased congruity" postulated by Osgood and Tannenbaum (1955) may be less closely related to Heider's concepts, the behavioral implications of this postulated tendency are similar. A recent variant of the consistency point of view is Festinger's "cognitive dissonance" (1957). All of the above approaches agree that there is a tendency for people to behave in ways which will maintain an internally consistent belief system. They differ, however, in their conceptions of consistency and the means by which it may be measured.

Two specific types of cognitive consistency are investigated in the studies reported in this chapter. One, "logical thinking," is the tendency for a person's beliefs (expectations) on related issues to be in accord with each other in the pattern required by the rules of formal logic. Previous research indicates that while the person's beliefs by no means follow the rules of formal logic perfectly, these rules do constitute significant predictors of human cognitive behavior (e.g. Woodworth and Sells, 1935; Thistlethwaite, 1950). The second kind of consistency dealt with in the present studies is one which we will call "wishful thinking." This is the tendency for a person's belief on a given issue to be in accord with his desire on that issue. Here again there is empirical evidence that such a wishful-thinking tendency is a partial determinant of belief (Lund, 1925; Cantril, 1938; McGregor, 1938).

In order to define operationally the distinction between wishful and logical thinking, the individual's belief system is regarded as being reducible to a series of propositions with which the individual can assent or dissent. Any one proposition tends to be logically related to others when it follows as a logical consequence from the others, or when these others follow as consequences of it. We consider the person to be thinking wishfully to the extent that his belief is founded on his estimate of the desirability of the proposition itself and of its consequences. (In common usage "wishful thinking" is often restricted to cases where desire interferes with reason.) A measure of wishful thinking is obtained in this study by asking the believer to indicate how desirable (regardless of truth or likelihood) he considers the state of affairs posited in the proposition to be. The person is considered, on the other hand, to be thinking logically to the extent that his belief on the given issue is in accord with his beliefs on related propositions from which the given belief follows as a logical consequence. We have attempted to develop a rather precise procedure for measuring logical consistency by the use of a formal "logic model" and associated measurement procedures.

THE LOGIC MODEL

Preliminary definitions. It will clarify the subsequent discussion if we define several terms at the outset. By a "cognition" we mean a response by which a person indicates his assent to the assignment of an event to a given position on a dimension of variability. "Event" here refers to any object of judgment, whether a physical entity, a behavior, an occurrence, a contingency, or a combination thereof (e.g. El Greco's "Toledo," my voting in the next election, man's reaching the moon, or the prohibition of swimming at public beaches). Possible "dimensions of variability" of such events would be their desirabilities, their likelihoods, etc. We use the term "beliefs" to refer to that subclass of cognitions which deals specifically with the likelihood dimension, and "wishes," to that which deals with the desirability dimension.

For the model developed below, we assume that the individual's beliefs have been obtained on a scale whose numerical values follow the axioms of probability theory. In practice, we have found it possible to obtain beliefs scaled probabilistically by presenting the respondents with appropriate propositions that assign the events in question to a position on the likelihood dimension (e.g. "man will reach the moon within the next ten years") and ask him to rate how true he believes the proposition to be. A line calibrated from zero to 100 is supplied and he is asked—after a brief discussion of the meaning of probability estimates in terms of betting odds—to make a mark on this graphic scale at the point where he believes the probability of the truth of the statement lies.

Consistency in initial levels of cognitions

The present model assumes that the person's belief space can be mapped in the form of propositions, $a, b, c \ldots k$, which locate events on some dimension of variability, and to which the person assents with some degree of subjective probability. The question of logical consistency arises when some relationship of formal logic can be established among sets of such propositions. As a paradigm in terms of which to discuss the model, we shall use sets of propositions related according to the following expression:

$$((a \cap b) \cup k) \to c, \qquad [1]$$

which can be verbalized as: "If a person assents to both a and b, or if he assents to k, then to be logical he must also assent to c." An example of a set of statements in this prototypical relationship would be:

    a. A major nuclear war would result in violent death to at least half the earth's population.

    b. A major nuclear war will occur within the next ten years.

    k. Factors other than nuclear war are going to result in violent death to at least half the earth's population within the next ten years.

    c. At least half the earth's population will meet violent death within the next ten years.

Expression [1] has been chosen for discussion because it is applicable to a wide range of behavior and readily lends itself to expansion so as to take into account more complex cognitive structures: e.g. any of the beliefs, *a, b,* etc., can be replaced by complexes of interrelated beliefs (see Appendix, p. 103).

We can ascertain the person's belief on any issue by asking him to indicate his assent to such propositions in probabilistic terms. His belief concerning *c,* for example, is his evaluation of the probability that this statement is true (p(c)). If an individual's beliefs are consistent, they should satisfy the following equation:

$$p(c) = p(a \cap b) \cup k) = p(a \cap b) + p(k) - p(a \cap b \cap k)$$
$$[2]$$

The minimum value that p(c) can take under any circumstances is p($a \cap b$) which equals p(a)p(b/a). Assuming that *a* and *b* are independent events, p′(c)—the logically required value of p(c)—becomes:

$$p'(c) \geq p(a)p(b) \qquad [3]$$

This equation will frequently be used in the subsequent experimental tests. The complete derivation of these formulae is given in the Appendix.

Consistency in changes of beliefs

Paradoxically, it is easier to specify the extent of changes in beliefs demanded by consistency than it is to specify the exact initial levels demanded. Even where it may have been impossible, because of the difficulty of measuring p(k), to measure the exact degree of consistency among the initial levels of the set of beliefs, it would be possible to use exact equations to evaluate the internal consistency of subsequent changes in these cognitions under the conditions typically obtaining in persuasive communication research. We have in mind here the experimental design involving measures of opinion before and after the presentation of persuasive messages, and the assumption that uncontrolled outside forces affecting the person's opinions on other relevant issues are small and uncorrelated during the interim. Alternative to this assumption a control, no-communication group can be used to provide a baseline that eliminates the effect of such outside forces. Under these conditions, the requirement for a consistent change of belief on the conclusion, $\triangle'\,p(c)$, becomes:

$$\triangle'\,p(c) = p(a)\,\triangle\,p(b) + \triangle\,p(a)p(b) + \triangle\,p(a)\,\triangle\,p(b) \qquad [4]$$

where $p(a)$ and $p(b)$ are the "before" beliefs and the troublesome $p(k)$ quantity (discussed in the Appendix) drops out of the equation.

Alternative methods of measuring consistency

We find in the published literature at least three separate approaches to the problem of measuring internal consistency among cognitions: the "face validity" method, the "population parameter" method, and the "formal model" method. The model described above is an example of the third procedure. In the paragraphs below, these three methods will be briefly described in terms of representative examples, and some of their contrasts will be indicated.

The face validity method. Perhaps the most commonly used criterion for cognitive consistency is the use of propositions so clear-cut that a set of cognitive responses to them is internally consistent or not almost by definition. This method is employed by Brehm (Chapter 5) and others. For example, Festinger (1957), following Kelman (1953), defines as inconsistent ("dissonant") the behavior of a pupil who is induced to write an essay favoring jungle comic books over superman comic books when he actually believes the latter to be superior. Such a valid-by-definition criterion has proved quite serviceable in many experiments, but its usefulness is largely confined to extreme cases of inconsistency, and it makes scaling degrees of inconsistency difficult.

The population parameter method. A more rarely used criterion of the internal consistency of a person's cognitions is the extent to which they conform to the modal pattern of cognitions found in the population from which the individual was drawn. In the study by Blau (1953), for example, opinions on foreign and domestic policies were found to be correlated within his respondents: people tended to favor participation in international organizations to the extent they favored labor unions. Hence a student who opposed American participation in international organizations but favored labor unions would be classified as having an inconsistent set of opinions. The possibly fallacious assumptions involved in defining intra-individual consistency by such an actuarial criterion are apparent. It is a testimony, however, to the power of the need for consistency that even so tortuous an index of consistency has proved a useful predictor of behavior (Blau, 1953; Berelson, Lazarsfeld, and McPhee, 1954; Hovland, Lumsdaine, and Sheffield, 1949).

The formal model method. This method is used, for example, when the subject is asked his opinion of the truth of three propositions that stand in a syllogistic relationship to one another: if he responds affirmatively to the two propositions that constitute the premises and negatively to the conclusion, he is classified as inconsistent on this set of opinions; any other set of opinion responses classifies him as consistent.

Some logical models using expressions more complex than the syllogistic have been used by Thistlethwaite (1950). Guilford et al. (1950, 1951), Green et al. (1953), and Morgan and Morgan (1953) have also used more complex materials, but the published form of the data does not permit easy comparison of the various expressions. More recently, Cartwright and Harary (1956), Abelson and Rosenberg (1958), as well as Osgood and Tannenbaum (1955) and Osgood, Saporta, and Nunnally (1956) have proposed models which are more generally applicable than the classical systems in two respects: (1) they make it possible to evaluate the internal consistency among a larger number of cognitions than are contained in the classic syllogism; and (2) they bring propositions which are not formally interrelated into logical relevance to one another by encoding the subject's response to all items according to some general plus-minus system.

One way in which the present formal model differs from previous models is in the precision with which it attempts to scale the cognitive responses by which the person indicates his assent to propositions. Whereas the models of Abelson and Rosenberg, Cartwright and Harary, and Osgood and Tannenbaum are basically two-valued (i.e. involve the application of simple plus or minus signs or, at most, a few more ordinally scale gradations), the present model attempts to provide a ratio-scaled index of the subject's belief by having him respond to the statement with a "subjective probability" estimate.

The logical model just presented attempts to overcome many of the shortcomings of previous methods of evaluating cognitive consistency. First, it allows us to judge the consistency of the individual's cognitions among themselves, without reference to the distribution of beliefs in the population. Second, by combining probability theory and formal logic, this model takes account of gradations in the person's commitment to particular cognitions. Thus, slight amounts of inconsistency can be measured, and the amount of inconsistency among a set of cognitions can be estimated.

Another difference between this model and some of the

other formal models is the way it handles the logical fallacies commonly made by humans. The relative merits of different strategies of treating this "common fallacies" problem are more a matter of taste than of intrinsic superiority. The model-builder has two alternatives; first, he can build some of the common fallacies into the model. For example, Abelson and Rosenberg's (1958) rule 3 intentionally violates the rules of the Aristotelian inductive analysis by allowing a conclusion—in fact, a positive conclusion—to be drawn from two negative premises. The related models of Heider, Newcomb, and Cartwright and Harary also integrate this fallacy into their models. Similarly, Abelson and Rosenberg's rule 2 works potential "undistributed middle" fallacies into the model. This approach suggests that these theorists aim to include all the commonly observed fallacies within the model itself, which then would be a behavioral, rather than a logical, model and no more internally consistent than behavior itself.

The alternative strategy, used in developing the scheme presented in this chapter, is to formulate a model that conforms to observed human cognitive processes, but only within the restriction that the rules of the model be logically consistent. Then we seek to handle the deviations of obtained behavior from the most appropriate internally consistent model by introducing additional postulates, such as the already mentioned one regarding a wishful-thinking tendency and others described in the final section of this chapter.

METHOD

Several experiments employing the model described above have been carried out to test a series of hypotheses about the consistency among a person's beliefs and wishes on a set of related issues. Since the methodology was essentially similar from experiment to experiment, we shall describe the general procedures at the outset and then present the results with respect to the successive hypotheses. Methodology will not be commented on further unless an experiment deviates from the general procedural paradigm described below.

Procedure. For each experiment, there were two sessions scheduled one week apart during regular academic class meetings. The study was typically represented to the subjects as a test to measure the effect of controversial materials on reading comprehension. In the first (before-communication) session, the subjects' cognitions regarding likelihood and desirability of sets of related events were measured. In the second session seven days later, the subjects were given persuasive messages arguing for the likelihood of certain of the events, and the subjects' postcommunication cognitions regarding likelihood and desirability of the events were measured. In some experiments, there was a third session one week later in which the cognitions were again measured (to determine the persistence of the communication-induced changes).

Materials. The cognitions were measured by questionnaires containing from 27 to 72 propositions. Among these propositions were a number of triads each of which constituted a "Barbara"-type syllogism—all A's are B's; all B's are C's; therefore all A's are C's. (One of the syllogistic triads used was the following: "Any form of recreation that constitutes a serious health menace will be outlawed by the City Health Authority." "The increasing water pollution in this area will make swimming at the local beaches a serious health menace." "Swimming at the local beaches will be outlawed by the City Health Authority.") The propositions making up any one syllogism were dispersed within the questionnaire, with the propositions from other syllogisms and filler items coming between them. The propositions concerned issues in which the subjects were felt to have at least a mild degree of involvement.

Beneath each proposition was a five-inch scale calibrated at half-inch intervals with the scores 0, 10, 20, . . . 90, 100. At the left of the scale were the words "very improbable end"; at the right, "very probable end." The subject was instructed to indicate his opinion of the truth of each proposition (without regard for his hopes or wishes on the matter) by drawing a line through the scale at the point where he felt the probability of its truth lay.

The desirability opinions were obtained by administering an additional questionnaire which listed all the propositions again, asking the subject to indicate his feelings regarding the desirability of the event posited in each proposition (without regard for likelihood or truth) by marking an X in the appropriate one of five response categories labeled from "very desirable" to "very undesirable."

The persuasive messages were reasoned appeals about 300 words long. Each message was attributed to a (fictitious) person with an institutional affiliation designed to enhance his perceived objectivity and expertness. Each message argued in favor of the truth of a proposition that constituted the minor premise of one of the syllogisms. In the typical design, any one subject received persuasive communications on some issues and furnished control (no-communication) data on the other issues.

Subjects. The subjects in two of the experiments were third- and fourth-year students in a large city high school; in the other two studies, freshmen in the general college of a state university were employed. The latter were mostly from the lower half of their high school graduating class in academic grade average. They were deliberately chosen so as not to represent a high degree of intellectual attainment or any familiarity with formal logic, since it was felt desirable to measure the consistency of cognitive behavior in subjects who were not consciously attempting to conform to any explicit formal logical model in their judgments. There were more boys than girls among the subjects, though both sexes were represented in all groups. The number ranged in the several studies from 35 to 130.

RESULTS

In this section, we will first discuss the tendencies toward logical and wishful thinking that were initially found in the subjects. Then we will discuss changes in beliefs from session to session with and without the experimental introduction of persuasive communications.

Initial levels of consistency

It was hypothesized that the initial levels of belief in logically related propositions would represent a compromise between logical- and wishful-thinking tendencies. Our criterion for logical thinking is conformity with equations [2] to [4] above, or those described in the Appendix; and for wishful thinking, agreement between hopes and expectations about events.

More specifically, the extent of logical thinking is given by the equation $p(c) \geqq p(a)p(b)$, where $p(c)$ is the subjective probability of the truth of proposition c, and $p(a)$ and $p(b)$, of propositions a and b, from which c is a logical consequent. In terms of descriptive statistics, the amount of logical thinking is given by the correlation between the set of truth ratings of the conclusions and the set of products of the truth ratings of the premises from which these conclusions respectively follow.[1] The statistic that describes wishful thinking, on the other hand, is the correlation between the truth rat-

1. This criterion assumes that the $p(k)$ values in equation [2] (discussed in more detail in the Appendix) are constant from argument to argument. That is, it assumes that each of the various sets of premises contributes about equal proportions of the total basis for accepting their respective conclusions.

ings and the desirability ratings of the propositions. A more adequate indication of logical thinking is furnished by the correlation between $p(c)$ and $p(a)p(b)$ when the truth ratings of the propositions are adjusted for their respective desirability ratings.

The data necessary for evaluating these tendencies were obtained in an experiment in which the subjects rated both desirability (on the 1-to-5 scale) and truth (on the probabilistic scale) of both premises and conclusion of 16 syllogisms (i.e. 48 propositions). In this experiment, indication of logical-thinking tendency was given by an obtained correlation of .48 (p = .06) between the probabilities of the conclusions and the joint probabilities of the premises of the 16 arguments (that is, between the $p(c)$ and the $p(a)p(b)$ values of the 16 syllogisms). Somewhat clearer evidence of logical thinking is given by the partial correlations between these two sets of probabilities when we adjust for the desirability ratings. The correlations between the conclusions' and the premises' subjective probabilities, with their desirabilities partialled out, is .85 (p < .01). This correlation is between the $p(c)$ and $p(a)p(b)$ scores of the 16 syllogisms, with the rated desirability of the conclusion and the mean of the desirability ratings of the two premises partialled out.

There is also evidence of a considerable amount of wishful thinking in these initial beliefs. The correlation between the truth and the desirability ratings on the 48 propositions was 0.40 (p < .01). The wishful-thinking tendency is also demonstrated by an alternative analysis: when the 48 propositions were partitioned on the basis of desirability, the mean probability rating of the 24 most desirable propositions was .55, while for the 24 least desirable, the mean was .46, a difference at the .03 level of confidence. The possibility that this positive relationship between the truth and desirability ratings of the propositions can be attributed to mechanical response sets on the part of the subjects is lessened by the use of quite different-appearing scales to measure the two dimensions. The truth scale was a continuous line calibrated in hundreths, while the desirability scale consisted of five discrete boxes to be checked. Moreover, the directions of the scales were reversed, with high probability at the right side and high desirability at the left.[2]

This obtained positive relationship between initial wishes and expectancies is, however, ambiguous as regards causal direction. It could be due to either (or both) of two tendencies, a wishful-thinking tendency, such that beliefs are assimilated to desires, or a rationalization tendency, such that desires are assimilated to beliefs. A study reported later in this chapter partially clarifies this ambiguity.

A correlation between expectancies and wishes does not necessarily represent cognitive distortion at all. Adjusting one's beliefs to one's desires may be quite rational, providing the person has any of a number of conceptual systems. For example, a Leibnitz who accepted the premises that this is the best of all possible worlds or that, at least, things generally turn out for the best, or that the universe is ruled by a perceptive and benign deity, is thereby acting rationally when he adjusts his beliefs to accord with his desires. Such adjustment would also be rational on the basis of a cognitive system that included postulates such as the following: People have some influence over the course of events; other people have much the same desires as I; people work to bring about outcomes they desire.

2. In generalizing the findings described by the correlations reported in this experiment, it should be observed that the scores on the basis of which these corrections were computed are mean scores based on groups of subjects. Hence they do not provide parameters that describe the behavior of individuals.

The Socratic method of persuasion

From the "need for consistency" postulate, it would follow that a person's beliefs on logically related propositions can be modified by the Socratic method of merely asking him to verbalize his beliefs, thereby sensitizing him to any inconsistencies among his beliefs, and thus inducing changes toward greater internal consistency. The contention that opinion change can be thus effected by the Socratic method calls for a considerable number of assumptions: (1) that people do have a need to maintain internal consistency among their opinions on logically related issues; (2) that inconsistencies may be introduced among such opinions by other inner needs, capacities, or external factors (such as wishful thinking or those discussed in the last section of this chapter); (3) that these inconsistencies tend to persist, despite the need for consistency; (4) that one basis for the maintenance of inconsistency is the cognitive isolation of these opinions from one another by logic-tight compartmentalization; (5) that pressure toward consistency can be applied to a person by making the "cognitive barriers" between these "compartments" more "permeable" and that merely stating his opinions on each of the related issues within a short time interval suffices to make permeable the barriers between the hitherto isolated cognitions. Perhaps the reason the effect of the Socratic method on beliefs has not previously been tested experimentally is that it depends on so many untested assumptions. The present experiment is an attempt to test predictions made on the basis of these assumptions.

In this experiment, 120 subjects were asked to indicate their beliefs on logically related propositions in one experimental session and again a week later, without having received any persuasive messages on the issues in the interim. It was hypothesized that the beliefs expressed in the first

session would be distorted in the direction of wishful thinking. It was further predicted that this first elicitation of beliefs would sensitize the subjects to inconsistencies, so that
an adjustment away from the wishful-thinking distortion
would be found in the second session. Additional hypotheses,
discussed below, dealt with the focus of the Socratic effect,
that is, with the question: When the subject is sensitized to
inconsistencies among his beliefs, which of the beliefs is most
likely to be adjusted to reduce the inconsistency?

In order to test the hypotheses, the subjects were asked to
rate the desirability of each of 48 propositions which constituted 16 syllogisms. On the basis of these desirability ratings, the 16 syllogisms were divided into two sets of 8. One
set included the syllogisms whose conclusions received low
desirability ratings relative to the mean of the two premises,
and the other set, those syllogisms with relatively desirable
conclusions. The auxiliary, wishful-thinking hypothesis
was confirmed in that, in the first session, the beliefs in the
truth of the propositions followed their desirabilities: for the
first 8 syllogisms, the probability of the conclusions exceeded
the product of the premises' probabilities by only 2.20 points
(on a 100-point "probability" scale), while for the second set
of 8 syllogisms the excess was 17.18 points.[3] This difference
of almost 15 points was significant at the .01 level.

According to the Socratic-effect hypothesis, the beliefs

3. While the difference between these two excesses, 2.20 and 17.18, is clearly
in the direction that accords with the postulated wishful-thinking tendency,
it might be thought that the absolute magnitude of the first quantity, 2.20,
is at variance with that tendency. Specifically it might seem surprising that
there is any excess probability at all for the relatively undesirable conclusions:
if expectance follows wishes, then should not the subjective probability of the
undesirable conclusions have been less than the product of the premises'
probabilities? That such a prediction does not follow can be seen when we
consider equation [2]. Any conclusion tends to follow, not only from the
experimentally utilized premises, but also from a variety of other premises,
so that there is a $p(k)$ value that tends to make $p(c)$ exceed $p(a)p(b)$, even
when the conclusion is quite undesirable as compared to the premises.

should be more internally consistent in the second session than in the first. In view of the wishful-thinking distortion just described, this increased internal consistency should take the following form. The relatively undesirable conclusions of the first 8 syllogisms should show an increase in probability ratings (relative to the premises) in the second session, while the relatively desirable conclusions of the second set of 8 syllogisms should show a loss of belief relative to the prem-

TABLE 6. *Correction in the distortions of the expectation opinions from the first to second administrations of the questionnaire*

	Mean change on major premise	Mean change on minor premise	Mean change on joint prob. of premises	Mean change on conclusion	Mean excess change on conclusions over premises
Syllogisms with conclusions less desirable than premises	−3.04	1.45	−0.79	5.17	5.96
Syllogisms with conclusions more desirable than premises	3.96	−1.98	2.06	0.35	−1.72

ises. Table 6 shows that the results bear out this prediction. The relatively undesirable conclusions showed a relative gain in belief rating of 5.96 points in the second session, while the relatively desirable conclusions showed a relative loss of 1.72 points in the second session. The differences between these changes is significant at the .02 level.[4]

4. It might seem that differential change in beliefs between the two sets of syllogisms could be due to a regression effect. It should be noted, however, that the syllogisms were partitioned on the basis of initial desirability, and not belief, ratings. But the initial split on the basis of desirability did indeed produce a corresponding initial difference with regard to excess belief in conclusions over premises (as might have been anticipated in view of the

Hence it appears that merely stating his beliefs on related propositions results in the respondent's adjusting these beliefs toward greater mutual consistency by the time he is asked to restate them again one week later, even without any experimentally introduced persuasive communication in the interim. It should also be noted that the question of belief consistency was in no way made salient to the subjects in this study. No mention was made of our interest in measuring cognitive consistency; the logically related propositions were widely dispersed within the questionnaire and the assessment of inconsistency involved quantitative computations unfamiliar to the subjects. Hence, for the operation of the Socratic effect, it seems sufficient merely to elicit the inconsistent beliefs with some degree of temporal contiguity: it is not necessary that the subject be conscious that his beliefs are inconsistent.

Since the inconsistencies found among the syllogistically related beliefs in the first session could have been reduced by appropriate alterations in any one or more of the three propositions, we tested several plausible-seeming hypotheses regarding the focus of the Socratic effect, that is, characteristics of a belief that made it particularly liable to adjustment in case of mutual inconsistencies with other beliefs. Three such characteristics were investigated: order of elicitation in the first session, desirability valence in the first session, and logical status within the syllogism. Only the last was significantly related to amount of change toward consistency.

---

positive relationship, described above, between belief and desirability ratings). Hence, a number of additional analyses were carried out to determine if there was evidence of a Socratic effect over and above the changes that could be expected on the the basis of regression. Perhaps the most convincing of these checks on a possible regression artifact was an analysis of covariance that adjusted the change in $(p(c) - p(a) p(b))$ scores on the basis of the initial levels of these scores and the within-groups correlation between initial levels and change. Even after such an adjustment, the differential mean changes between the two sets of syllogisms remain significant $(.02 > p > .01)$.

The mean change toward consistency was greatest on the major premises (3.50), next greatest on the conclusions (2.41 points), and least on the minor premises (−1.71, that is, a change away from consistency). An over-all analysis of variance indicates that the differences among these means is significant at the .05 level.

Clearly, the nature of this difference is that the major premises and conclusions contribute more to the change toward consistency than the minor premises (p = .03). By logical analysis, the common characteristic of the majors and conclusions that distinguishes them from the minors is inclusion of the predicate term of the syllogism. For example in the syllogism given previously, the predicate term is "outlawed by the City Health Authority." Since in this type of Barbara syllogism the predicate term tends to be the most emotionally charged, it may well be the most significant contributor to initial distortion and hence it is not surprising that the adjustment back to consistency produced by the Socratic method focuses on it.

Rationalizations consequent upon induced belief changes

As was discussed earlier, the obtained correlation between beliefs and desires is ambiguous in regard to causal direction—either wishful thinking or rationalizing or both could account for it. A complete design for determining which of these tendencies is operative would involve experimentally inducing (1) a change in desirability and measuring any consequent change in belief (indicating wishful thinking) and (2) inducing a change in belief and measuring any consequent change in desirability (indicating rationalization). In terms of the system for mapping cognitive space discussed above, a change of belief on a given proposition could be induced by communicating a persuasive message arguing for the increased likelihood of its logical antecedents. A change in its desirability, on the other hand, could be induced by communicating a persuasive message arguing for the increased desirability of its logical consequents.

The relevant experiment carried out in the present program did not employ the full design but only the half that allowed detection of rationalization. That is, we experimentally induced increased beliefs in propositions by communicating persuasive messages that argued for increased beliefs in premises from which the given beliefs would follow. The consequent changes in the desirabilities of the given propositions were then measured.

Eight syllogistic arguments were used in this study. The truth and desirability of each of the 24 propositions were rated by 92 subjects, as described in the methodology section. One week later the subjects received messages arguing for the increased likelihood of the minor premise of each syllogism. These messages said nothing about the desirabilities of these propositions or about the likelihood or desirability of the conclusions.

The effects of these messages on the desirability ratings are shown in Table 7. In all cases the communications argued for the increased likelihood of the propositions. Both changes in the desirability ratings of the premises themselves and of the unmentioned conclusions that followed from them show the effects of rationalization. The premises themselves were judged more desirable by subjects receiving the likelihood messages than by the control subjects not receiving any messages (p. = .02). The conclusions also show an increase (p = .08) in desirability after receipt of the messages, though the change in desirability on the implicit conclusions is, as might be expected, less sizable than the change on the explicit premises. Such as it is, this change on the unmentioned conclusions indicates that the rationalizing tendency extends even to logically related issues not explicitly mentioned in the persuasive message. From these results it is reasonable to conclude that at least part of the correlation between wishes and expectations is determined by rationalization. The re-

TABLE 7. *Rationalization tendencies; desirability ratings of the explicit premise and of the derived unmentioned conclusion after receiving a message arguing for the likelihood of the premise (Experimental Group) or after not receiving such a message (Control Group)* *

Issue †	DESIRABILITY OF EXPLICIT PREMISE		DESIRABILITY OF UNMENTIONED CONCLUSION	
	Control	Experimental	Control	Experimental
1	1.35	1.26	1.37	1.17
2	1.56	1.21	1.58	1.19
3	1.97	1.67	1.50	1.54
4	2.36	1.65	2.28	1.87
5	2.99	1.95	2.99	2.10
6	3.71	3.82	3.65	3.80
7	2.84	2.15	2.95	2.56
8	1.60	1.63	3.08	3.04
Mean	2.32	1.92	2.42	2.16

* High numerical scores indicate *low* desirability.

† Issue numbers refer to separate sets of syllogistically related propositions. The complete texts of these propositions and of all the persuasive messages used in conjunction with them have been deposited with the American Documentation Institute. Order Document No. 6235 from ADI Auxiliary Publications Project, Photoduplication Service, Library of Congress, Washington 25, D.C., remitting in advance $1.25 for microfilm or for photocopies. Make checks payable to Chief, Photoduplication Service, Library of Congress.

sults do not rule out the possibility that the reverse, wishful-thinking tendency is also involved, but no experiment in the present program has tested this alternative factor.

Resistance to inconsistency-increasing messages

If a person has a tendency to maintain consistency among his beliefs, he should be highly susceptible to persuasive messages arguing in an inconsistency-reducing direction and highly resistant to those that increase inconsistency. This hypothesis has already been suggested by Festinger (1957), who found some experimental corroboration for the prediction. In the present experiment we employed as an auxiliary hypothesis to identify initial inconsistency the postulate that beliefs would be distorted by wishful thinking, so that relatively desirable propositions would receive inconsistently high beliefs. Specifically, if the conclusion of a syllogism is rated as more desirable than the premises, then it was postulated that the conclusion's probability would be rated inconsistently high as defined by equation [3]. Hence, a message that argued for the probability of a premise that received a high desirability rating relative to that of its conclusion would be pushing the person in an inconsistency-increasing direction and would, we hypothesized, be strongly resisted. A message arguing for the truth of a premise that had been rated less desirable than its conclusion, conversely, would be pushing the person in an inconsistency-decreasing direction and hence make a relatively large persuasive impact.[5] That is, we are predicting that (at least where the question of consistency is even mildly salient) it is easier to convince the individual of the likelihood of undesirable, rather than desirable, states of affairs.

5. Alternatively, we might have defined initial inconsistency of the likelihood ratings directly in terms of the initial obtained likelihood ratings, a procedure adopted by Festinger (1957, Chapter 9). In this way the syllogisms whose initial $p(c)$ values were high relative to their $p(a)$ $p(b)$ values would be defined as having premises whose initial likelihood ratings were inconsistently low, while syllogisms whose initial $p(c)$ values were low relative to their $p(a)p(b)$ values would be defined as having premises with inconsistently high initial likelihood ratings. The more indirect definition (in terms of the rated relative desirability of premises and conclusions) was used because the direct definition assumes that the $p(k)$ values (see Appendix for discussion) are constant from syllogism to syllogism, while the indirect definition assumes only that the $p(k)$ values are unrelated to the relative desirabilities of premises and conclusions.

To test these predictions, the subjects were asked to rate 24 propositions, constituting eight syllogistic triads, as to likelihood and desirability. The premises of four of the syllogisms were rated more desirable than their conclusions and those of the other four were rated as relatively undesirable. The subjects were then given persuasive communications arguing for the increased truth of one premise (the minor) of each syllogism. It was predicted that these messages would have less effect on the relatively desirable premises than on the undesirable minor premises. The prediction was borne out by the data (see Table 8).

TABLE 8. *Resistance to inconsistency-producing messages*

Issue *	CHANGES IN LIKELIHOOD OF PREMISES RATED MORE DESIRABLE THAN THEIR CONCLUSIONS		Issue	CHANGES IN LIKELIHOOD OF PREMISES RATED LESS DESIRABLE THAN THEIR CONCLUSIONS	
	Immed. after message (change from before)	*One week after (change from immed. after)*		*Immed. after message (change from before)*	*One week after (change from immed. after)*
1	18.56	−12.97	5	18.56	−13.86
2	11.07	−4.29	6	27.13	−9.56
3	7.14	−3.15	7	26.06	−14.99
4	20.71	−10.00	8	22.85	−18.92
Mean	14.37	−7.60	Mean	23.65	−14.34

* See footnote to Table 7.

The immediate effect of the messages was to increase the truth ratings of the desirable premises 14.37 points on a 100-point scale, while the undesirable premises showed an increase of 23.65 points, the difference being significant at the .01 level.[6] That this difference is not due to a regression effect

6. This greater tendency to increase the rated likelihood of an undesirable premise more than that of a desirable one might seem like dissonance-increasing behavior. However, it should be noted that while such a tendency

is shown by the fact that the difference remains significant at the .01 level even when the corresponding changes in a no-communication control condition are used as a baseline for computing communication effects.

It was further predicted that the inconsistency-reducing changes brought about by the messages would be more persistent than the inconsistency-increasing changes—because the former would be stabilized by the anchoring effects of the related, consistent beliefs. The data do not support this prediction (see Table 8). Of the 14.37 points of change induced on the desirable premises, 7.60 points were lost during the week after the persuasive communication; while of the 23.65 point change induced on the undesirable premises, 14.34 points dissipated during the ensuing week. Hence in terms of absolute loss the prediction is reversed, and in terms of proportion lost of the originally induced change, both sets of propositions show about equal decay rates. This failure to find any greater persistence of induced changes in an inconsistency-reducing direction is discussed further when a similar disconfirmation is found in the study reported below.

Remote effects of persuasive communications

Most of our beliefs tend to be logically related to other beliefs and therefore, on the postulate of a tendency to maintain internal consistency among beliefs, a persuasive message that is effective in changing our belief on an explicit issue should change our beliefs also on related issues which (even though not mentioned explicitly in the message) are logically derivative from the explicit propositions. Hence, it was predicted

---

does increase the discrepancies between the expectations and desires, it is decreasing the discrepancies between expectations and expectations. Some suggestion as to why there should under the present experimental conditions be a reduction in the latter discrepancies, even at the expense of an increase in the former, is offered by the "salience" postulate discussed in a later section of this chapter.

that persuasive messages change beliefs not only on the explicit issue but also on unmentioned logically derivative issues.

It seems reasonable, however, to postulate that this consistency tendency will not be perfectly realized in actual cognitive behavior. Hence, two limiting corollary effects were hypothesized. First, it was predicted that the change on derivative unmentioned issues would be less than that logically required (by the size of the change induced on the explicit issue and equation [4], described above). Further, it was predicted that a second limitation in cognitive consistency would be a degree of temporal inertia because of which the persuasive impact of the messages would filter down to the derivative issues only gradually after receipt of the messages.

To test these hypotheses 120 subjects participated in three experimental sessions. In the first they indicated their belief in the truth of each of 16 syllogistically related sets of propositions. In the second session, about one week later, they received persuasive messages arguing for the truth of each of the 16 minor premises (the majors and the conclusions being unmentioned) and then indicated their immediate postcommunication belief in each of the 48 propositions. In a third session, one week after the communications, the subjects again indicated their beliefs in the propositions (thus providing an indication of the persistence of the initial impact of the message).

The immediate postcommunication impact on the explicit and the derived issues are shown in Table 9. It can be seen that a mean change of 17.56 points was induced on the explicit issues (the minor premises), a change significant at the .01 level. The unmentioned logically related issues (the conclusions) also showed a change, 5.96 points, in the consistent direction (.01 < p < .02). Hence, the basic hypothesis, that the messages have an effect on unmentioned but logically related issues, is confirmed. (These changes are for the subjects receiving the persuasive messages, from a baseline provided by control, no-message subject. This baseline was used to eliminate regression effects.)

TABLE 9. *Changes from before to immediately after the persuasive communications*

	Change on explicit target issue (premise)	Logically required change on derived issue (conclusion) *	Obtained change on derived issue (conclusion)	Discrepancy of obtained from required change on derived issue
Mean	17.56	11.57	5.96	−5.61
Sig. level	p<.001	p<.001	.01<p<.02	.02<p<.05

* Logically required change on conclusion is equal to $\triangle$ p(a) p(b) + $\triangle$ p(b) p(a) + $\triangle$ p(a) $\triangle$ p(b). See text for fuller discussion.

Table 9 also shows the logically required change on each conclusion as prescribed, according to equation [4], by the obtained changes on the premises from which it follows. It can be seen that the logically required change on the derived unmentioned issues, 11.57, is considerably less than the change obtained on the explicit issue. However, as predicted, the obtained change on the derived issue is 5.61 points less (.02 < p < .05) than the relatively small required amount, confirming the hypothesis that changes on the remote issues, while significant, are significantly less than the logically required amount.

The temporal inertia hypothesis (that the communication impact would filter down to remote issues only gradually) receives some support from the results (see Table 10). During the postcommunication week a loss of 8.43 points of the originally induced 17.56 points occurred on the explicit issue. Some loss did occur also on the derived unmentioned issues (the conclusions) but these changes were small—only 1.48

points—as compared with the 6.69-point change logically required (by equation [4] and the obtained loss on the explicit issues). The last column in Table 10 shows that there was 5.20 points greater retention (p = .10) of the induced change on the derived issue than would be predicted in view of equation [4] and the size of the obtained decay on the explicit premise. This greater retention on the derived issue suggests

TABLE 10. *Changes from immediately after to one week after the persuasive communication*

	Change on the explicit target issue (premise)	Logically required loss on the derived issue (conclusion)	Obtained loss on the derived issue (conclusion)	Excess retained gain over required on derived issue (conclusion)
Mean	−8.43	−6.69	−1.48	5.20
Sig. level (t-test)	.02>p>.01	.05>p>.02	.70>p>.60	p = .10

that, as hypothesized, the originally induced change on the premise continued to filter down to the conclusion during the ensuing week and partly overcame the temporal decay of persuasion on the derived issue. Similar suggestions of a delayed action effect on derived issues have been reported by Hovland, Lumsdaine, and Sheffield (1949) and Stotland, Katz, and Patchen (1959).

The basic finding—that the messages have an impact on logically related issues not mentioned in the communication—conflicts with the results reported by Hovland, Lumsdaine, and Sheffield (1949), Hovland and Mandell (1952), and Cooper and Dinerman (1951), which suggest that persuasive messages have little or no effect on derived issues. The derived impact is particularly striking in the present study in view of the fact that the messages did not even make explicit all the premises needed for the derivation of the conclusion, but only the minor premise. In the Hovland and Mandell study all the material necessary for the derivation of the conclusion was presented in the message, and still very little remote impact occurred.

A number of factors may account for the more positive findings regarding remote effects in the present study. Though the conclusions were not mentioned in the messages they did all appear on the lengthy opinion questionnaire presented to the subjects during the first session, one week before the communication, and this questioning may have increased the salience of the derived issues. Also, there was a more precise measure of change in the present study than in the earlier ones, thus facilitating detection of the derived change, even though the expected change on the conclusion (as defined by the consistency model) was small compared with the obtained change on the explicit issues.

Remote impact as a function of initial inconsistencies

Still other hypotheses were tested that dealt with the extent the message impact on logically related but unmentioned conclusions was affected by the initial distortions of belief. On the basis of the postulate that people resist an increase in cognitive inconsistency, it was predicted that the persuasive message would have a greater effect on a derived unmentioned conclusion to the extent that the message argued in a direction that tended to push the belief on the explicit issue (the premise) into greater inconsistency with that derived conclusion. To the extent the message was arguing in such a direction on the explicit issue, the person would become increasingly inconsistent unless he changed his opinion on the derived (unmentioned) issue also.

To test this hypothesis we once again employed eight sets

of syllogistically related propositions, with the subjects first asked to indicate the desirability and likelihood of each proposition. On the basis of the desirability scores, the syllogisms were partitioned into the four with relatively undesirable conclusions and the four with relatively desirable ones. As before, initial distortion was identified in terms of wishful thinking: it was postulated that for the first four syllogisms the initial beliefs on the (relatively desirable) premises would be inconsistently high relative to those on the conclusions; while for the second four, the reverse would be the case.

In a second session one week later the subjects were given persuasive messages, each arguing for increased belief in the minor premise of one of the syllogisms. Hence for the first four syllogisms the messages were arguing in an inconsistency-increasing direction, while for the second four they were arguing in an inconsistency-decreasing direction. Therefore, according to the prediction that the subjects would respond to keep inconsistency at a minimum, the remote impact of the messages on the derived unmentioned issues (the conclusions) should have been greater in the first four syllogisms than in the second four.

This prediction is borne out by the results shown in Table 11. The relatively undesirable conclusions of the first four syllogisms show an immediate derived impact of 11.15 points, while the relatively desirable conclusions of the second four show an immediate derived impact of only 1.70 points on the 100-point scale. This difference is significant beyond the .05 level.

It was further predicted that this greater impact on the undesirable conclusions would be more lasting than the effects on the desirable conclusions, because of the bolstering effect of the consistent beliefs. The results shown in Table 11 give no support to this prediction: the inconsistent remote changes (i.e. the increased beliefs in the desirable conclusions) are actually slightly more persistent than the consistent changes.

TABLE 11. *Remote impact (on logically related but unmentioned conclusions) of messages arguing for increased likelihood of premises* *

	CHANGES IN LIKELIHOOD OF THE UNMENTIONED RELATIVELY UNDESIRABLE CONCLUSIONS			CHANGES IN LIKELIHOOD OF THE UNMENTIONED RELATIVELY DESIRABLE CONCLUSIONS	
Issues †	Immed. after message (change from before)	One week after (change from immed. after)	Issues †	Immed. after message (change from before)	One week after (change from immed. after)
1	14.63	−23.38	5	9.64	1.81
2	4.29	− 4.64	6	12.14	−11.66
3	12.14	2.79	7	0.35	− 5.35
4	13.56	− 1.78	8	−15.35	− 1.07
Mean	11.15	− 6.75	Mean	1.70	− 4.07

* Messages aimed at syllogisms with relatively desirable premises (that is, relatively undesirable conclusions) are inconsistency-producing; and those aimed at relatively undesirable premises (that is, relatively desirable conclusions) are inconsistency-reducing.

† See footnote to Table 7.

The disconfirmation of this prediction of greater stability for consistency-increasing changes on the derived issues, together with the disconfirmation (reported in an earlier section of this chapter) of the similar prediction of greater stability of the consistency-increasing changes on the explicit issues, suggests that beliefs are compromises between two potentially conflicting tendencies: wishful and logical thinking. Thus the initial states of beliefs represent a compromise between consistency with desires and consistency with evidence. The persuasive messages upset the balance by presenting new evidence and, in general, making the evidential realm of the cognitive universe momentarily more salient. Hence, the immediate postcommunication effect is the adjustment of beliefs toward greater consistency with the evidence, i.e. with beliefs on logically antecedent issues. Once the person is out of the communication situation, however, the initial, globally determined balance tends to reassert itself with the result that the beliefs shift back toward desires, and the logically consistent induced changes, while initially greater, are, if anything, less stable than the logically inconsistent ones.

To maximize the utility of a consistency postulate in accounting for cognitive behavior we have to recognize that cognitive consistency is not just a matter of logical thinking—of consistency between belief and belief on related issues—but also a matter of wishful thinking, that is, consistency between belief and desire on the same issue. Experimental manipulations can make one or the other of these consistency tendencies momentarily more salient and thus effect a temporary shift either toward or away from logical consistency.

FURTHER SOURCES OF BELIEF INCONSISTENCY

Most of the hypotheses discussed above were based on two postulates: a person tends to minimize logical discrepancies between belief and belief on related issues, and between belief and wish on the same issue. Following a somewhat arbitrary convention, we have referred to the former tendency as "consistency-producing," and the latter, as "distorting." In this final section we shall review various factors, in addition to the wishful-thinking tendency stressed in this chapter, that tend to distort beliefs and hence introduce logical inconsistency within the individual's belief system. Two classes of distorting factors will be considered successively: (1) forces other than, and potentially in conflict with, the logical consistency tendency which shape a person's beliefs and (2) structural limitations within the cognitive apparatus which tend to prevent a person's achieving complete logical consistency.

Forces conflicting with cognitive consistency

Inconsistent samples of information. Inconsistency among beliefs can derive from a person's dependence, in forming his beliefs, on the available information, of which he may have an incomplete and even incorrect sample. There being reasons for and against almost any stand on any issue, a person may receive in one context a sample of information that, say, supports the premises and, in another, information tending to refute a logically derivative conclusion. The resulting inconsistency in this example should take the form of an excessive $p(c)$ value, that is, $p(c)$ would be greater than $p((a \cap b) \cup k)$.

Attributed adherents. It has been frequently demonstrated that a person tends to accept a cognition when he is given to believe that the cognition is adhered to by a prestigeful person (Hovland and Weiss, 1951), or by a positive reference group (Kelley, 1955), or by "everyone" (Moore, 1921; Asch, Block, and Hertzman, 1938), or when it is labeled with some respected term ("democratic," "fair," etc.) (Birch, 1945). Conversely, a person tends to reject a cognition when a negatively valenced adherent is attributed to it (Osgood and Tannenbaum, 1955). Hence, another way inconsistencies can be introduced into the person's cognitive system is by attributing differently valenced adherents to premises and to conclusions.

Response stereotypy. Studies of behavior on judgmental tasks have revealed a number of tendencies which result in the clustering of responses at certain points on a scale (Cronbach, 1946, 1950). Such response stereotypes could well produce manifest cognitive inconsistencies under specifiable

conditions. There are, for example, position biases that produce response clustering near the top of a vertical and the
left of a horizontal scale (Mathews, 1927). Also well known
is the "generosity" bias that results in a concentration of responses toward the favorable end of the scale. In addition,
there is a tendency to polarize beliefs (Osgood and Tannenbaum, 1955) and a contrary tendency to pile up responses at
the midpoint of the scale (Lorge, 1937). In the case of such
opposite tendencies, each of which has evidence in its support, a more complex theoretical synthesis must be sought. It
may be that frequently used cognitions tend toward the extremes, while infrequently used cognitions tend to be con-
centrated toward the middle of the scale (Brim, 1955). Any
such tendency for all cognitions to gravitate toward a single
point on the scale or in a single direction would introduce
apparent inconsistencies into the belief system. Another form
of response stereotypy that could produce manifest inconsistencies is the various patternings that tend to emerge in a
serial judgmental task. There are possible assimilation and
contrast effects whereby a judgment tends to be distorted
toward a preceding response which is similar, and away from
a dissimilar preceding response (Hovland, Harvey, and Sherif,
1957). There may also be a tendency to balance a set of
judgments so as to make approximately equal use of all the
response categories allowed. The type of inconsistency introduced by such patterning tendencies would depend on such
idiosyncratic features of the task as the order in which the
propositions are presented.

Flaws in the cognitive apparatus

So far we have considered some sources of cognitive inconsistency due to other factors operative in belief formation
which might conflict with, and partially override, the tendency toward consistency. Now we shall consider some addi-

tional sources of inconsistency which arise from observed inadequacies in the cognitive apparatus itself and which, therefore, permit inconsistencies in cognitive behavior even in the absence of conflicting forces.

Compartmentalization. The appearance and persistence of cognitive inconsistency in the individual indicate a degree of "logic-tight" compartmentalization in the human thinking apparatus, by virtue of which certain sets of cognitions can be maintained isolated from one another, without regard for their logical interrelatedness. Studies on authoritarianism and rigidity have suggested there are detectable individual differences in the degree to which people tend to maintain such cognitive barriers impermeable—and therefore have a potential for cognitive inconsistencies (O'Connor, 1952). To cite a familiar example, ability to remain impaled on what Myrdal (1944) calls the "American dilemma" (subscribing to egalitarian principles and yet denying equal rights to ethnic minorities) seems to require a degree of cognition rigidity and impermeability. But in addition to relatively persisting personality differences in levels of logic-tight compartmentalizing, there are situational factors that might be expected to affect a person's ability to maintain such compartmentalization. Most obviously, being forced to state a set of opinions explicitly in close temporal contiguity should tend to lessen the possibility of maintaining these opinions out of relation to one another and consequently should reduce the potential for maintaining inconsistencies in the set of opinions. A derivation from this analysis is tested in the Socratic-effect experiment described above.

Logical inertia. Also tested in the experiments described above are two types of cognitive distortion that can be expected on the basis of a postulate that beliefs tend to be somewhat anchored, so that a certain amount of force must be expended just to overcome the stationary inertia. First, we can postulate that the individual's chain of reasoning is best represented by a "loose-link" or "elastic" model, with a certain amount of give or stretch. Hence, some finite increment of change in a cognition is necessary before any pressure for consistency is exerted on the logically related propositions. We would expect, with such a loose-link cognitive structure, that the obtained levels of cognitions on related issues would deviate from the consistency model increasingly as the most direct logical relationship between the cognitions comes to involve increasing numbers of mediating links (or propositions). Also, an induced change in one cognition would be expected to be felt progressively less than prescribed by the consistency model as we proceed through the successive steps of a logical chain.

A second implication of the inertia model is that there would be an increasing time lag before the effects of an induced change in one cognition has its full impact on a person's more distantly related cognitions. These inertial factors are postulated as characteristics of the cognitive process per se, independently of the above-mentioned forces conflicting with consistency. Where such conflicting forces (e.g. wishful thinking) are also operative, they would further augment the attenuation and time lag produced by inertia (Thistlethwaite, 1950).

Logical fallacies. Studies of human performance of inferential thinking tasks have revealed a number of deviations from the logical model which occur with sufficient frequency to be called "logical fallacies." Some of these fallacies are perhaps more a consequence of the peculiarities of the experimental task than of human cognitive behavior in the usual natural situation. In this category would fall the frequent errors (Lefford, 1946) due to the subject's inability to make the distinction required in the usual syllogistic reasoning task between the truth of a conclusion and its validity.

Also in this methodological category of fallacies are errors resulting from the "ambiguous some." The experimenter, following logical convention, defines "some" as meaning "some or all"; the subject often defines it as "some but not all" and hence in the case of an argument that permits a universal conclusion, subjects tend (Wilkins, 1928; Sells, 1936) to reject as invalid the particular conclusion which follows a fortiori from the universal premises in the Aristotelian logical model.

Of more interest are the logical fallacies in observed behavior that are less task-specific. There is the "wariness" factor, first reported by Wilkins (1928), which is a tendency to reject strong conclusions even when valid—"strong" here being defined as affirmative rather than negative, and universal rather than particular. Also very common, particularly when the task involves abstract material (Morgan and Morton, 1944), is the "atmosphere effect" (reported by Woodworth and Sells, 1935; and Sells, 1936): a tendency to make a response similar to the earlier, given components of the task. In reasoning tasks this effect takes the form of overrating the validity of conclusions of the same quantity or quality as one or both premises and underrating the validity of conclusions differing in quantity and quality from a premise. This tendency would be most pronounced in what we might call the "bandwagon" situation where we have two premises of the same quantity and quality (for example, two A—universal affirmative—premises). In such situations there is a strong tendency to overrate the validity of a conclusion of the same quantity and quality. (For example, in the case of premises like "all x's are z's, all y's are z's," the atmosphere effect would produce an erroneous tendency to judge "all x's are y's" as valid, although it is invalid by reason of "undistributed middle.")

It might also be economical and behaviorally meaningful

to encode inconsistencies in syllogistically related sets of cognitions in the categories of one of the classical typologies of reasoning errors (e.g. undistributed middle, illicit process of major). Wilkins (1928) has attempted an empirical count of the relative frequency of such categories of errors. There are also fallacies that we might expect from the ambiguities of our language, for example, equivocal terms, amphibolous constructions, and composition and division of collective nouns. The availability of alternative systems for classifying reasoning errors provides a potentially useful tool for evaluating theoretical models for cognitive processes. We can draw up sets of fallacious arguments that are differently ordered by the several models as regards the number of logical errors they involve. The ordering of such arguments with respect to frequency of obtained errors would give some indication of the kind of cognitive surveillance system that is actually employed by humans engaged in reasoning problems.

It seems indicated by the program of experiments described in this chapter (and by those described elsewhere in this book) that the tendency to maintain logical consistency among one's cognitions is neither nonexistent nor absolute. This tendency and other potentially—often actually—conflicting tendencies each account for significant portions of the obtained variance in human cognitive behavior. The current trend in psychological research toward increasingly greater interest in the rational component of cognitive behavior does not, therefore, represent a closer approach to reality. (Indeed, the current psychological trend is reversed in philosophy, which shows a mounting interest in irrational relative to rational processes.) We see in this trend the inevitable reversal of perspective that marks scientific progress: theorists and researchers in any area for a time tend to concentrate on exploiting the creative potential provided by one approach until diminishing returns set in, and there then occurs a re-orientation which offers a fresh reservoir of creative stimulation. It appears that we have arrived at the point in our present state of knowledge when it is becoming more profitable for the time being to exploit the concept of man as rational, and we thus find students of cognitive behavior making increasing use of the cognitive consistency concept.

A "Logic" Model for Belief Consistency

THE EMPIRICAL WORK described in this chapter was carried out to test several hypotheses regarding consistency among beliefs and among induced changes in beliefs. Consistency was defined by means of a "logic model" that described how interrelated beliefs, if consistent, would behave with respect to one another. This appendix discusses several aspects of that model, including the assumption involved, the derivation of the equations, its application to the empirical data, and some further extentions of it.

It is assumed that a person's belief space can be mapped by means of propositions, a, b, . . . t, that assign objects of judgment to a position on some judgmental dimension such as that of desirability or likelihood. Further, it is assumed that the person's belief on any such issue can be measured by having him indicate, in terms of subjective probability, his assent to the appropriate proposition, these probability responses being termed $p(a)$, $p(b)$, . . . $p(t)$, respectively. The empirical work dealt with subsets of beliefs which included propositions related in the form of the expression: $((a \cap b) \cup k) \rightarrow c$.

Restricting the discussion to expressions of this form still allows fairly general applicability of the model to the totality of belief sets since it is understood that a, b, k, and c are not necessarily atomic but may stand for combinations of expressions of the same form as the given expression or for their negations, or for the null case. Hence both the expression to the left and to the right of the implication sign can be considered functionally complete, since any belief can be introduced into the system, and more than enough operators ($\cap$, $\cup$, $\rightarrow$, and in effect, negation) are provided, implicitly or explicitly, for a functionally complete system. However, the discussion is restricted to sets of beliefs in an antecedent-consequent relationship. In the final paragraphs of this appendix, the possibility of extending the model to beliefs in relations other than the antecedent-consequent is discussed.

In order to relate this expression to probability theory, several additional definitions were introduced. Two of these definitions were $p(c/(a \cap b)) = 1$ and $p(c/k) = 1$, which require that c be a necessary inference from $(a \cap b)$ and also from k. The system can, however, be readily generalized to situations where $(a \cap b)$ implies c with any degree of probability, $p(i)$; and k implies c, with $p(j)$. A third definition was $p(c/(\sim (a \cap b) \cap \sim k)) = 0$, that is, if neither $(a \cap b)$ nor k obtained, then c could not possibly occur. This definition also is simply a convenience, lumping all the logical antecedents to c, except the experimentally interesting $(a \cap b)$ into a single (possibly complex) symbol, k. A fourth definition states that $(a \cap b)$ and k are mutually exclusive, that is, $p((a \cap b) \cap k) = 0$. The fifth states that a and b are independent, i.e., $p(a/b) = p(a)$. All the probabilities referred to here are subject probabilities, which are assumed by the present model to behave according to the axioms of probability theory.

With these definitions, we can derive equation [3] above, $p'(c) \geq p(a) p(b)$, which was utilized in formulating a number of the experimental predictions described in that chapter. We could, however, dispense with these definitions in the interest of generalization, at the cost of more complicated equations. Eliminating definitions 4 and 5 regarding mutual exclusiveness and independence, the equation for a logically consistent $p(c)$ would become $p'(c) = p(a)p(b/a) + p(k) - p(a \cap b \cap k)$. Or eliminating definition 1 and 2, regarding necessity of implication, $p'(c)$ becomes equal to $p(a)p(b)p(i) + p(k)p(j)$. Likewise we could eliminate the third definition by atomizing k into any number of component propositions which imply c, in which case we would introduce all the first order and interaction terms into the equation, giving terms with odd numbers of factors a positive sign and those with even numbers of factors a negative sign. For example, if c is implied by (and only by) r or s or t, then the logically required level of $p(c)$ is $p'(c) = p(r) + p(s) + p(t) - p(r \cap s) - p(r \cap t) - p(s \cap t) + p(r \cap s \cap t)$.

Hence the use of the more restrictive definitions was not an intrinsic requirement of the model, but rather adopted for reasons of economy. We decided that the model and the associated hypotheses could be more conveniently tested by the tactic of using the restrictive definitions and selecting experimental material that would meet their special requirement.

The $p(k)$ difficulty. Equation [3], $p'(c) \geqq p(a)p(b)$, is less satisfactory than we might wish because it specifies exactly only the lower limit of a logically consistent $p(c)$, rather than its precise value. Nevertheless, it was decided to utilize this asymmetrical expression rather than the exact equation—$p'(c) = p(a)p(b) + p(k)$—in the experimental work because of the difficulty of empirically determining the $p(k)$ value. We have defined $p(k)$ as the subjective probability of occurrence of all states of affairs, other than the conjunction of a and b, that would imply c. There are several approaches to an empirical determination of the $p(k)$ value.

One approach (already discussed in another connection) involves attempting to map exhaustively the individual's cognitive space with respect to beliefs, say $p(r)$, $p(s)$, $p(t)$, that would imply the given belief, $p(c)$. In this situation, where $(r \cup s \cup t) \rightarrow c$, and $(\sim r \cap \sim s \cap \sim t) \rightarrow \sim c$, then the requirement for a consistent $p(c)$ would be:

$$p'(c) = p(r) + p(s) + p(t) - p(r \cap s) - p(r \cap t) - p(s \cap t) + p(r \cap s \cap t)$$

As was pointed out above, this equation can be generalized to situations involving any number of propositions that imply c by introducing all the first order and interaction terms and giving positive signs to terms with odd numbers of factors and negative signs to those with even numbers of factors.

When there are so many premises from which c would logically follow that it is not feasible to measure the persons beliefs on each of them, or when it is not possible to determine whether all possible premises have been identified, then we may attempt to measure p(k) nonspecifically, by asking the person his belief on a proposition of the form: "Even if a or b were not so, c would still be the case." (The example of a k proposition given on page 68 would permit the measuring of p(k) in this nonspecific way.) Such a procedure would permit use of the exact equation, but a p(k) so determined might lack psychological meaningfulness.

Alternatively, when we are dealing with several sets of beliefs, each of which contains beliefs in the ($(a \cap b) \cup k) \to c$ relationship, we can handle this p(k) difficulty by assuming that the p(k) value is constant from set to set. (We thereby assume that the a and b premises we have selected are about equal, from set to set, in the proportion of the total probability of the conclusion for which they account.) In such cases, we can specify that p(c) is directly proportional to p($a \cap b$) as the requirement for logical consistency, and specify that any set of cognitions exhibits internal inconsistency to the extent that it departs from the overall regression line of p(c) on p($a \cap b$). This procedure was followed in some of the empirical work reported in Chapter 3.

Actually, for most of this empirical work, it was not necessary to make so demanding an assumption as the equality of the p(k) values; it was necessary only to assume that these values were uncorrelated with the independent variable being manipulated, for example, with the desirability of the conclusion relative to the premises. An assumption of this type is made in experimental work whenever we use only a sample of material. It is assumed that this sample is "typical" in the sense of being adequate in range and representativeness to justify generalizing the outcome to a whole universe of materials. Since it would be impractical, if not impossible, to enumerate completely all possible arguments in the form ($(a \cap b) \cup k) \to c$ and then select a random (or otherwise representative) sample of them for the empirical work, this assumption is rather gratuitously made though, unfortunately, no more than is usual in experimental work. Generalization in science is intrinsically risky.

Should it be known a priori that the person's beliefs on the issues are internally consistent, then p(k) could be computed from the empirically determined values of $p(a)$, $p(b)$, and $p(c)$. However, such a computation is likely to be of little use since the internal consistency of the person's cognition, far from being a valid a priori assumption, is usually just what we want to evaluate.

Defining consistent changes in beliefs. As has been pointed out above, the difficulty of empirically determining the $p(k)$ value is readily circumvented when we assess the logical consistency, not of the initial levels of related beliefs, but of the experimentally induced changes in these beliefs. It is possible to design persuasion experiments so as to eliminate net changes in $p(k)$. We may employ a large sample to minimize any systematic extraneous influence sufficiently to assure that only small and uncorrelated $\triangle p(k)$'s occur from person to person during the experimental period. In this case, the $\triangle p(k)$ value approximates zero and hence drops out of the $\triangle' p(c)$ equation. Alternatively, we may employ a "control" group which is given no experimental manipulation to provide a baseline that allows us by statistical procedures to eliminate any $\triangle p(k)$ effect.

This convenient circumvention of the $p(k)$ problem when dealing with contemporaneous changes in related beliefs is possible only within the restricted situation obtaining in the empirical work described in Chapter 3. All of this work dealt with the experimental induction of a change in an antecedent belief and then the observation of the subsequent change in the consequent. As far as the equations of the model for consistency are concerned, the expected changes in the antecedent subsequent to an induced change in the consequent should be strictly analogous to those in the reverse direction. That is, equation [4] of Chapter 3 should hold not only where the induced change is in $p(a)$ or $p(b)$, but also when it is in $p(c)$. However, some new methodological problems arise when we induce changes in the consequent and observe whether the predicted changes in the antecedents follow.

In the first place, while we can easily induce a change in $p(a)$ or $p(b)$ without explicitly mentioning one of the derivative beliefs, $p(c)$, it might seem more difficult to induce a change in this conclusion, p(c), without discussing explicitly the antecedents which lead to it. Hence, it might be suspected that any change in p(a) or p(b) attendant upon an induced change in p(c) is an artifact resulting from the necessary mention of a and b (or some other antecedents) in the course of inducing the p(c) change. However, the psychological literature indicates strongly that it is possible to manipulate belief concerning c without any mention of the associated propositions from which it follows. For example, in the work described by Rosenberg in Chapter 2, changes in specific beliefs are induced by affect manipulation, without any mention of related beliefs. Also, the work on wishful thinking, discussed above, indicates that the subject's belief in the likelihood of c can be manipulated by discussing the desirability of c or of its logical consequents without any mention of the likelihood of its antecedents. Hence the methodological problem of testing the adequacy of the consistency model for changes induced in the reverse direction (that is, from consequent to antecedent) are not insurmountable as far as manipulating the consequent without explicit mention of the premises is concerned.

A somewhat more serious problem that arises in testing the model's adequacy for these reverse-directional changes concerns the research design for handling the p(k) difficulty. It has already been pointed out that by using a large sample and the usual assumption of small and uncorrelated changes in experimentally uninteresting variables or by the use of suitable control groups, this p(k) difficulty can be circumvented when comparing the changes on the conclusion that are associated with induced changes in the antecedents. The circumvention is not so easy, however, when we measure the changes on the antecedents associated with an induced change in the conclusions. The problem here is analogous to the problem of predicting the course a piece of wet spaghetti will follow across a table when we pull it as opposed to when we push it. The person can maintain internal belief-consistency between a conclusion and its antecedents, following an induced change of belief on the conclusion, by changing his belief on any one or several sets of antecedents from which the conclusion would follow. Even if we can assume, somewhat gratuitously, that the adjustment will be divided equally among the various sets of antecedents, we are still confronted by the tactical drawback that the predicted change of belief in any given antecedent (for example, $p(a \cap b)$) to be expected as a result of an induced change of belief in its consequent ($p(c)$) will be less than the predicted change in the other direction.

Further extensions. In principle, the model described here for defining consistency can be easily extended to handle sets of beliefs in relationships other than that of implication. Setting up an empirical situation in which these extensions can be tested, however, introduces some formidable additional methodological problems. One rather general extension that seems capable of testing involves "co-ordinate" propositions, that is, propositions which are related, not as antecedent-consequent, but as co-consequent of the same antecedent. For example, the following two propositions, "Military expenditures will decrease in 1961" and "In 1961 restrictive legislation regarding labor unions will be enacted," could be co-consequents of antecedents including the common proposition, "A Republican will be elected president in 1960." A belief system showing a logical relation between these two propositions would be the following:

a1. The election of a Republican president in 1960 would result in lower military expenditures in 1961.

a2. The election of a Republican president in 1960 would result in the enactment in 1961 of legislation restricting labor unions.

b. A republican will be elected president in 1960.

k1. There will be lessened military expenditures in 1961 for reasons other than (a1, b).

k2. There will be restrictive union legislation in 1961 for reasons other than (a2, b).

c1. Military expenditures will decrease in 1961.

c2. In 1961 restrictive legislation regarding labor unions will be enacted.

By having the person indicate his adherence to each of these propositions in subjective probability terms, and by using the definitions described in the early paragraphs of this Appendix, we can prescribe that a logically consistent p(c1) would equal p(a1) p(b) + p(k1) and p'(c2) would equal p(a2) p(b) + p(k2). By solving each equation for p(b), substituting and solving for one of the conclusion-beliefs, we can specify how the beliefs, p(c1) and p(c2), on these co-effects should be related if the person is to be initially consistent, namely:

$$p'(c1) = \frac{p(a1)}{p(a2)} \ [p(c2) - p(k2)] + p(k1)$$

It can be seen in the above equation that the p(k) difficulty in determining consistent initial levels is even more pronounced with beliefs in a co-ordinate relationship than in the already dis-cussed case of inferentially related beliefs. With co-ordinate be-liefs, there are two such quantities, p($k1$) and p($k2$) to be con-sidered. Furthermore, they enter into the consistency equation with different signs so we cannot even set up so simple a general asymmetrical equation as was possible with the case of the in-ferentially related beliefs. The methods for empirically deter-mining p(k) which were discussed in that earlier case do remain relevant here also.

When we proceed to the problem of defining consistency for contemporaneous changes in beliefs which are in a co-ordinate relationship, we find that the situation is analogous to that with inferentially related beliefs, though somewhat more complex. More specifically, the analogy is with the situation where a change is induced on the conclusion and we have to define the logically required amount of change on the premise. With co-ordinate beliefs, we have, in effect, to define the logically required impact on the common premise as a result of the induced change on the one conclusion and the required impact of this premise change, in turn, on the other co-ordinate conclusion.

Were we able to induce a change on one of the co-ordinate conclusions and to hold constant (by some control procedure or experimental design) all the antecedent beliefs except that on the premise common to the two conclusions—p(b) in the example above—then the logically required change on the other co-ordinate conclusion can be simply defined as:

$$\triangle'\mathrm{p}(c1) = \frac{\mathrm{p}(a1)}{\mathrm{p}(a2)} \triangle\mathrm{p}(c2)$$

It is unlikely that we can in practice meet this requirement of holding constant beliefs on all antecedents of the co-ordinate conclusions other than their common premise. However, the equation becomes more empirically testable when the change is experimentally induced on the common premise, and the comparative resultant changes on the co-ordinate conclusions are evaluated. This co-ordinate-conclusion case is only one example of the possible extensions of the model and of the resultant difficulties entailed in its empirical testing.

CHAPTER 4

An Analysis of Cognitive Balancing

MILTON J. ROSENBERG AND ROBERT P. ABELSON

THE CONCEPT IN PHYSICAL SCIENCE of "field stability" or "equilibrium" has spread to, and been incorporated by, the biological and psychological disciplines. The basic conception common to all versions and uses of this concept is simply that when a number of entities or processes are mutually interactive there will be some state or states of optimum order toward which such interaction tends; once such a state is achieved, the magnitude of activity characterizing the "system" in which the entities or processes are contained will be reduced.

Reworkings of this concept to suit the needs and conceptual categories of systematic psychological inquiry are visible in the theorizing of such diverse figures as McDougall, Freud, Pavlov, Hull, Tolman, Lewin, and many others. Whereas some of these authors tended to emphasize its applicability, via "homeostatic" formulations, to the motivation-learning interaction, Lewin (and to some extent, Tolman, as well as other more conventional Gestalt psychologists) attempted to build a "psychology of knowing" upon the basis of the equilibrium concept.

Background

Certain directions pointed by Lewin's ambitious, but sometimes ambiguous, theoretical approach toward a psychology of knowing have been sharpened and creatively developed in the recent work of Heider (1946, 1958). The specific phenomena which Heider seeks to explain are those involved in the development and stabilization of "interpersonal perceptions." His theory "deals with how one person feels about another person—how o is represented in the life space of p— and especially the positive and negative character of this representation, that is, p's, liking or disliking o; it also considers how this liking or disliking is influenced by things or other persons to which o is related in some way, or which in some way belong to him" (Heider, 1958).

Heider's approach to this problem is based upon the principle that the sentiment (affect) characterizing one's response to a person will tend toward "balanced" relation with the sentiment characterizing one's response toward some object (e.g. condition, event, goal, other person) with which the person is perceived to be related. Thus if p likes object x and other person o either likes or "belongs with" object x, p will tend to like o; comparably if p dislikes object x and other person o either likes or "belongs with" object x, p will tend to dislike person o. In the case in which o and x are seen to be in negative relationship it is expected that p will tend to feel negative toward x if he is positive toward o, or positive toward x if he is negative toward o. In its most generalized form this axiomatic assertion is simply that beliefs about another person will become stabilized when the three "signs" involved in such a belief (p toward o, p toward x, and o toward x) are either all positive or two of the three are negative. Any such set of three signs will be unstable if one or three of the signs are negative. Clearly then, Heider's theory postulates that cognition (in the sense of perceived relationships) tends to be consistent with affect (in the sense of feelings toward persons and other "objects").

A basic, predicted consequence of a person experiencing an unstable interpersonal cognition (i.e. an inconsistency between beliefs and feelings) is that further cognitive operations will be attempted until over-all sign changes are achieved by which the cognition becomes "balanced" and thus stable. Evidence in support of predictions derived from this proposition is scattered diffusely among a large number of studies. We shall briefly review several of these.

In a study executed by Esch (reported in Heider, 1958) subjects were asked to predict the probable outcomes of various "unbalanced" social situations. One typical situation was presented in these terms: "Bob thinks Jim very stupid and a first-class bore. One day Bob reads some poetry he likes so well that he takes the trouble to track down the author in order to shake his hand. He finds that Jim wrote the poems." In response to this dilemma (in which p dislikes o, likes x, and discovers that x "belongs with" o) and similar ones, the outcomes predicted by the subjects involved changing the sign of p's feeling toward o, toward x, or of his belief about the real relation between o and x. Virtually all such changes were of the sort which "resolved the disturbance" (i.e. transformed the situation into a balanced one in which either all three signs are positive or two are negative and one is positive).

Another example of what Heider has designated as the "preference for balanced states" is provided in an experiment by Jordan (1953). Two hundred and eight subjects were required to indicate their preferences for various "triadic situations" stated in an abstract form which merely indicated "liking relations" and "unit relations" between p, o, and x. Some of these were balanced situations and some

were not. The former received significantly higher preference ratings than the latter. Reinterpreted by Cartwright
and Harary (1956), Jordan's data were shown to yield still
stronger verification of a preference for balance than was
originally claimed.

A study by Kogan and Taguirri (1958) demonstrated the
applicability of the balance hypothesis to sociometric data
collected from groups of naval personnel.

Newcomb has reported a series of interesting studies
(1953, 1958) in which a "strain toward symmetry" (balance
between cognitions) is evidenced in correlations between
subjects' ratings of the "importance" of issues and their expectations as to how both liked and disliked persons would
rate those same issues. Similar evidence is provided in an
experiment reported by Horowitz, Lyons, and Perlmutter
(1951). Indeed, the general balance proposition here under
consideration has been so frequently tested for its bearing
upon interpersonal perception that a brief review such as
this one cannot presume to cover the literature. A useful,
but by no means exhaustive, review is available in a recent
volume edited by Taguirri and Petrullo (1958), though many
of the contributions contained therein are focused not only
upon the balance hypothesis but upon other, and sometimes
unrelated, matters.

Beyond the demonstration that a preference for balance
exists, a few recent experiments suggest that from it there
can be predicted the cognitive directions that subjects will
pursue in filling out incomplete or ambiguous interpersonal
perceptions. One such study is that by Morissette (1958) in
which evaluations of unknown persons by a known and liked
person are shown under certain conditions to exert strong
influence (consistent with the balance hypothesis) upon the
subject's expectations toward the unknown person.

Since Heider's theory is probably the one that has guided

most of the studies reviewed above (though some seem to be more closely tied to the related formulations of Festinger, 1957; Newcomb, 1953, 1959; and Osgood and Tannenbaum, 1955) and since it is the one to which our own approach is most closely related, we shall frame three critical points in a way that bears primarily upon the body of work stemming from that theory.

The first of these points is simply that no systematic research program has been generated by Heider's model; what is available might be described as observational data consistent with the main lines of his thought (though by no means matching its rich extension to various classic and important problems) plus experimental data consistent with the simple broad principle of balance. No set of experimental manipulations is suggested. The main finding is simply that the balance principle, like other Gestalt principles, operates widely and must be considered an important determinant of ideational dynamics; experiments indicating the conditions and limits of its operation have not been reported.

A second lack is simply that the main body of recent research on cognitive balance processes, whether carried out by Heider's followers or others, is concerned almost *solely* with interpersonal perception. However, the balance principle upon which Heider's model is constructed is not inherently limited to the special case of interpersonal perception but seems rather to have direct bearing upon all cognitive processes in which the objects "cognized" are of affective significance to the "cognizer."

Still another limit is that the model is not extended beyond the *p-o-x* triad to parallel the complexities of structure found in real cognitive process. Typically persons think about affectively significant objects (be they persons or something else) in terms of their separate relations to some plural number of other objects or standards (some of which, furthermore, are thought of as they in turn relate to each other).

The work reported in this chapter attempts to penetrate beyond these three limits. The studies reported are experimental in form, tying in with the literature on persuasion and attitude change, and also involve some innovations in methodology which may be of interest for their own sake. The theoretical notions tested in these experiments essay a balance-formulation of "attitudinal" (i.e. affectively significant) cognitions generally and do so with reference to more complex cognitive structures than the triadic one studied in most of the recent research on interpersonal perception. There are still other ways in which our approach is unlike Heider's but the continuity of the one with the other (a continuity more emergent after the fact than in the actual work of developing the theory or designing the experiments) has required that this chapter begin with a brief review of his and related contributions.

A Model of Attitudinal Cognition

The experiments presented in this chapter are closely related to a general model of the dynamics of attitudinal cognition published earlier by the authors (Abelson and Rosenberg, 1958). Accordingly, it is desirable to review some portions of the earlier article. The treatment at the outset is essentially parallel to Heider's, but later branches out.

Cognitive elements. Human thought, for all its complexity and nuance, must involve some cognitive representation of "things," concrete and abstract. These things or concepts are the elements of our system. Though it does not seem absolutely necessary, we shall for convenience assume that individuals can attach some sort of verbal labels to the elements of their thinking. We shall refer, then, to cognitive elements by verbal labels.

Cognitive relations. Of all the conceivable relations between cognitive elements, we choose to consider only three: positive, negative, and null. These will be denoted p, n, and

o. We again conveniently assume that cognitive materials of a relational sort can be verbally labeled. Some typical examples of relations between elements follow:

positive (p)	negative (n)	null (o)
likes, supports	dislikes, fights	is indifferent to
uses, advocates	opposes, undermines	is not responsible for
possesses, aims for	inhibits, aims against	
helps, promotes	hinders, opposes	does not affect
is equivalent to	is alternative to, counteracts	
brings about	prevents	does not lead to
serves, is vital to	is inimical to	does not interest
justifies	obviates	cannot ensue from
is consistent with	is incompatible with	is unconnected to

Similar examples are given by Osgood, Saporta, and Nunnally (1956) in a slightly different context.

Certain omissions from the above scheme may occur to the reader. Relations like "is next in line to," "is north of," etc. are certainly not included. Other phrases which imply relationship without specifying its sign, e.g. "is related to," "has to do with," etc., are difficult to classify. As for other exceptions to the scheme, their phrasing tends to be affectless. Dispassionate descriptions of, say, the mating habits of flamingos or the economic situation in Vietnam would contain many relations impossible to classify. But such descriptions are reportorial, not attitudinal. When cognition is invested with affect, when the elements are responded to emotionally, then the relations become classifiable in terms of the present system. Our intent is to be able to code all relations occurring in attitudinal cognitions into these three broad categories. In so doing we do not duplicate Heider's distinction (1958) between "unit relations" and "sentiment relations."

Cognitive units. Cognitive units (or "bands") are built out of pairs of elements, connected by a relation. That is, the basic "sentences" of attitudinal cognition are of the form, ArB, where A and B are elements and r is a relation. Many sentences which at first seem more complicated than the simple ArB unit may be reduced to such a unit by broadening the definition of an element. For example, consider the sentence, vintage 1956, "Nasser (A) insists on (p) all Suez tolls (B) belonging to (p) Egypt (C)." (Here p denotes a positive relation.) This sentence, symbolically, is Ap(BpC). But regard (BpC) as a new element D, the broader conception "all Suez tolls belonging to Egypt." Then we have simply ApD. In this way, we reduce our catalog of basic sentences to three: ApB, AnB, AoB.

Cognitive balance and imbalance. Cognitive bands or sentences in "attitude structures" usually have the property that both of the concepts involved are of affect-arousing significance. If a concept eliciting positive affect is represented with the symbol +, and a concept eliciting negative affect with the symbol — (replacing the neutral A,B, . . . terminology), the set of basic sentences admits six patterns. Each pattern may be classified as either "balanced" or "unbalanced."

A balanced band is one in which the relationship asserted between two signed concepts is *consistent* with their signs. We predict as the major consequence of balance that the cognitive band will be stable; that it will be comparatively resistant to change. Specifically then, a balanced band is one in which either:

1. two concepts of identical sign are believed to be positively related (+p+ or —p—)

   or

2. two concepts of opposite sign are believed to be negatively related (+n—)

An unbalanced band is one in which the relationship asserted between two signed concepts is *inconsistent* with their signs. We predict as the major consequence of imbalance (when the person is *attending* to that imbalance) that the cognitive band will be unstable; that it will be comparatively likely to undergo change in a balancing direction. Specifically an unbalanced band is one in which either:

1. two concepts of identical sign are believed to be negatively related ($+n+$ or $-n-$)

or

2. two concepts of opposite sign are believed to be positively related ($+p-$).

When two affectively signed concepts are connected by a null relation there is by definition an absence of a cognitive band; though it should be acknowledged that under certain types of supporting conditions the person may feel a force toward finding a relation between the two concepts. It would be expected that this force would direct him specifically toward selection of that relational sign which would establish a balanced rather than an unbalanced cognitive unit. This process, *induction of new relations,* must be clearly distinguished from processes having to do with the resolution of existing imbalance. The authors' early article (1958) fails to make this distinction clear. The reader is referred to the study by Morrisette (1958) for a treatment of the problem of induction of new relations.

It should be clear that what we designate as a single band is equivalent to Heider's triadic grouping of relations between *p, o,* and *x.* Where we fix an affective sign to each of the two concepts in a band, Heider's notation indicates a "sentiment" relation extending from *p* to either *o* or *x.*

While our definitions have been limited to balance and imbalance in single cognitive bands, our original formulation (Abelson and Rosenberg, 1958) dealt not with these so much as with balanced and unbalanced attitudinal-cognitive structures. By structure we meant simply any plural number of bands in which each band is connected with (shares one concept term with) at least one other band. In this earlier publication we developed the concept of the "structure matrix," from which it is possible to determine an index of the degree of imbalance in a complex structure. We attempted to show also that it is possible to identify the *least effortful* path toward total balance, under the crude assumption that all changes in cognitive structure are equally effortful. (A somewhat parallel development has recently been given by Harary, 1959.)

Redressing imbalance. It is assumed that the general tendency to reduce or redress cognitive imbalance applies not only to interpersonal cognitions but to attitudinal cognitions generally. It is important to note, however, that potential imbalance will remain undiscovered by an individual unless he is motivated to think about the topic and in fact does so. Assuming these necessary preconditions, let us suppose that an individual does come upon a cognitive inconsistency in his attitude. What can he do about it? Three things:

1. Change one or more of the signs (in a single band the affect signs of either of the two concepts or the sign of the relation between them).
2. Redefine or "differentiate" one or more of the concepts.
3. Stop thinking.

A simple example will illustrate the first two methods. The third is self-explanatory. Take the two elements: C, Having Coeds at Yale; and G, Getting Good Grades. The subject might tell us,

"I'm for having coeds at Yale." (C is a + element)

"I want good grades." (G is a + element)

"Having coeds at Yale would undoubtedly interfere with getting good grades." (CnG)

This attitudinal cognition, reduced to the form of a simple cognitive band, is:

Coeds at Yale	would interfere with	getting good grades
+	n	+

Clearly the cognition is unbalanced. Never having been forced to take a consistent stand on the issue, however, our subject may readily tolerate (or even be unaware of) the imbalance. Now suppose that the issue is hotly debated and our subject thinks. The imbalance is encountered and motivates a search for a balance-producing resolution.

Method 1. He alters any one of the three signs, by weakening the desire for good grades, by opposing the admission of coeds, or by rationalizing to the effect that "coeds do not really interfere with getting good grades (in fact, they enhance the chances of getting good grades, etc.)."

Method 2. (The following is one of various possibilities.) He differentiates the concept "getting good grades" into "getting A's" and "getting C's" and then reasons that while coeds may interfere with getting A's, they do not interfere with getting C's, and what he really wants is not to get A's but to get C's.

It is assumed that under sufficient pressure to continue thinking, the individual will try methods 1 and 2, presumably seeking a relatively effortless means to achieve balance. If these attempts fail, because certain signs are resistant to change and certain elements are difficult to redefine, the individual may resort to method 3, which is to stop thinking. If, however, strong pressures, internal or external, do not permit him to stop thinking, he will re-examine the topic, seeking a more complex utilization of either or both of the first two methods and if this fails he will re-examine yet again. With extremely strong pressure to continue thinking, some cognitive units will in all probability ultimately yield to one attack or another. With weak pressure and a structure that is highly resistant to change, the individual will most likely stop thinking; his attitude structure will remain in the state it happens to be in at the moment, or possibly revert to some earlier state, but will, at any rate, be held beyond the range of active awareness and examination.

Thus we envision an extensive hierarchy of cognitive solutions to the problem of reducing imbalance. Experimental prediction of outcome is extremely difficult and constitutes a considerable challenge.

The experiments reported in the next section represent an initial attempt at studying ideational processes in terms of the balance-seeking force as it interacts with aspects of cognitive structures. The final section of the chapter presents a more refined analysis of the mechanisms available for effecting structure changes in the search for balance.

RESEARCH EVIDENCE

The two investigations reported in this chapter are concerned with the state of affairs in which a person, starting with an unbalanced cognition or set of cognitions "thinks" his way through to the achievement of an altered cognition or set of cognitions which either meets or fails to meet the requirements of our formal definition of cognitive balance. In each of these studies the subject's thinking is guided by his exposure to new information which he is required to evaluate and which he may reject or incorporate either in some partial, or in full, degree.

Thus, in general terms, these studies are ones in which

subjects are observed as they adapt to the presence, in their own thinking, of certain cognitive dilemmas. Variations in the dilemmas with which the subjects must cope are intended to represent certain factors which are hypothesized to be important in shaping the extent of subjective tension experienced and the direction the subject will take in attempting to reduce such tension.

STUDY 1

An explanation of our general methodology is required as a preliminary to presenting the first study. To enable grouping and comparison of subjects it was necessary to "implant" *identical* cognitive dilemmas in large numbers of persons. To accomplish this end each subject received a mimeographed pamphlet which began with a statement that the experiment was concerned with "how well you can play a certain assigned role." The role was then defined in terms of certain feelings and beliefs which, taken together, constituted a cognitive structure with some built-in dilemma. It will be convenient to defer the statement of the major hypothesis tested in the first study until the details of this method are more fully described and explained.

Method and predictions

All subjects were Yale undergraduates. Each was given a pamphlet whose first page informed him:

> This is an experiment in how well you can put yourself into another person's position and deal with the problems that this other person might face. You will be told what some of this man's basic values are. Then some information and a real-life problem will be presented. Try your very best to respond to the problem situation as this other person would—try to *be* this man.

The instructions then went on to define the assigned role as that of "the owner of a large department store in a middle-sized, Midwestern city." Three affective reactions toward three separate concepts, respectively, were provided as part of the content of the assigned role. The first of these, communicated to all subjects, was that as owner of the department store he placed a high positive value on "keeping sales at the highest possible volume in all departments of your store." The subjects in the first of three groups were also assigned to feel positively toward modern art and toward Fenwick, the manager of the rug department. In a second group, the assigned role required the subject to feel negatively toward modern art but positively toward Fenwick. In the third group the subjects were required to feel negatively toward both modern art and Fenwick. The subject's understanding and achievement of the role requiring these evaluative responses were checked by his response, in role, to evaluative scales referring to the three concepts "high sales volume," "modern art," and "Fenwick."

The assigned role (i.e. the assigned cognitive structure) also involved "beliefs" about the relations between these three concepts. Thus each subject was given further instructions to the effect that, as store owner he also held the following beliefs: Displays of modern art in department stores *reduce* sales volume; Fenwick *plans to mount* such a display in the rug department; Fenwick in his tenure as rug department manager has *increased* the volume of sales.

"Facts" known to the subject in his role as owner of the department store and supporting each of these three beliefs, respectively, were presented as part of the initial communication. Thus, in support of the belief that displays of modern art in department stores reduce sales volume each subject was told:

One year ago a report by the Merchandising Institute appeared in a leading market research journal. It warned against modern art exhibits in stores merchandising popular household products to lower and middle-class customers. The conclusions were based on a thorough and well-conducted research study which found that 55% of a representative sample of American consumers did not like modern art. Probably it was this basic attitude which underlay the further finding that 46% were offended or distracted by modern art displays and thus tended to spend less time and money in stores featuring such displays.

In support of the belief that Fenwick plans to mount such a display in the rug department the subject was told:

Fenwick told you yesterday that he is planning a modern art display in his rug department. He seems rather interested in this project and has even devoted a little of his spare time to developing its details. He estimates that he can have the display ready and mounted in about six weeks.

Supporting the belief that Fenwick in his tenure as rug department manager had increased the volume of sales the following was communicated:

An independent firm of auditors each year computes for the store a set of indices of comparative sales volume on the basis of which the various departments are ranked for relative effectiveness in selling their particular products. The year before Fenwick took over the rug department it ranked fifteenth in sales volume out of thirty-four departments. During the three years in which he has managed the rug department it has risen to fifth rank in sales effectiveness.

The order of presentation of the three paragraphs was randomized within each of the three experimental groups.

In this first study then, each subject was given a role defined in terms of his having a "triangular" cognitive structure consisting of three "bands" (i.e. a believed positive or negative relation between two concepts, each of which is either positively or negatively evaluated). In this experiment, the structures are "closed" ones: i.e. change on any band may have consequences for contiguous bands. Also it should be noted that, by assigning to each of the three groups cognitive structures identical in asserted relations but varying in the evaluations of the things related, the following condition is accomplished: each of the three structures is unbalanced but the locus of imbalance varies. In the first structure, with all concepts positively evaluated, it is the band involving the belief that modern art *hurts* sales that is unbalanced (+n+). In the second structure, with modern art negatively evaluated, the band involving the belief that the positively valued rug department manager plans to display modern art is unbalanced (+p−). In the third structure, with both modern art and Fenwick negatively evaluated, it is the band involving the belief that Fenwick has increased rug sales in the immediate past that is unbalanced (−p+). The three structures are displayed in Figure 2.

Each of the three structures may be transformed into a balanced one (i.e. a structure containing three balanced and no unbalanced bands) in a number of ways. The simplest (or "least effortful") approach would be to change the sign of the relation in the single unbalanced band. Thus in the first structure, with all concepts positively evaluated and positive relationships between Fenwick and sales volume and Fenwick and modern art, changing the relation between modern art and sales volume from negative to positive would achieve a balanced structure. However, other ways of balancing are possible. For example, the subject may change the positive relation between Fenwick and modern art to a negative one and then proceed to change his direct evaluation of modern art from positive to negative; or the subject may change the perceived relation between Fenwick and sales volume to nega- tive, change his evaluation of Fenwick to negative, and his

Figure 2. The Three Experimental Structures

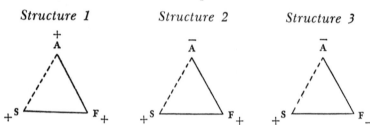

S denotes the concept "sales"; A, "modern art display"; and F, "Fenwick." Signs attached to these symbols indicate the initial valuations of the con- cepts by subjects assigned to the three structure groups. Dotted lines indicate negative relations between concepts, solid lines positive relations.

evaluation of modern art to negative. It is clear that if one examines the paths toward balance which are opened up by changing each of the three asserted relations respectively, each of these changes will represent a different level of further cognitive work (i.e. further effort expended in changing ad- ditional concept evaluations and/or perceived relations be- tween concepts).

The basic hypothesis tested in this first study was the fol- lowing: *The order of preference for paths toward restoring an unbalanced structure to balance will correspond to an ordering of the paths according to the number of sign changes required, from the least to the most.*

To test this hypothesis each subject was trained on one of the three structures described above. In all, 99 subjects went through the first phase of the experiment. Thirty-four were trained on the first structure, 33 on the second, and 32 on the third (see Figure 2).

Of the 34 trained on the first structure 12 failed to "internalize" that structure with complete accuracy. Eight of these subjects distorted the initial information in such a way as to avoid the imbalance. Thus when, after reading the structure-establishing communications, they were tested on scales calling for evaluation of the three concepts and the relations between them, they judged modern art displays as *fostering*, rather than reducing, sales volume. In so doing they achieved "prematurely balanced" structures, i.e. they eliminated the imbalance implied in the assigned negative relation between two affectively positive concepts. This is similar to the performances of the subjects in the study by Esch, reviewed above. The remaining 22 subjects in this group were able to conform to the role assignment; they were able, in role, to reproduce the beliefs and feelings that, taken together, constituted the first of the three experimental structures.

Only one of the 33 subjects assigned to the second structure, and 4 of the 32 subjects assigned to the third structure, failed to reproduce the structures accurately. Interpretation of the fact that more "premature balancing" occurred with the first structure than with either of the others will not be attempted here. The meaning of this fact will be clear in the light of an emergent proposition developed below.

The subjects who failed to reproduce the structures on which they had been trained were eliminated from the experiment, and the remaining subjects went on to read three communications that were represented as issuing from three different store officers, each of whom had something to say about the "general situation" involving the rug department. One of these communications (the Art-Sales or AS communication) contended that modern art displays actually *increase* sales volume. A second communication (the Fenwick-Art or FA communication) argued that Fenwick really does *not* plan to display modern art in the rug department. A third communication (the Fenwick-Sales or FS communication) argued that Fenwick really has *failed* to maintain sales volume in the rug department. Each communication presented "evidence" in support of its basic assertion. Thus, each subject was exposed to three communications any one of which, if accepted, could serve as the beginning of a process of cognitive change which would restore the total structure to balance; but accepting one of these three communications would involve only one sign change, while accepting the others would require two or three sign changes, depending upon the structure and the communication.

Thus the primary prediction was that the communication which would make possible the balancing of a particular structure through only one sign change would be the most acceptable of the three communications for subjects trained in that structure. A secondary prediction was that, of the two other communications, the one implying two sign changes to reach balance would be better received than the one implying three sign changes. Thus it was specifically predicted that for subjects trained on the first structure the Art-Sales communication would be most acceptable; for those trained on the second and third structures the most acceptable communications would be Fenwick-Art and Fenwick-Sales, respectively. The secondary prediction specified that for structure 1, Fenwick-Art would have more appeal than Fenwick-Sales; for structure 3, that Fenwick-Art would have more appeal than Art-Sales. For structure 2, both nonappropriate communications imply two changes and thus there is no differential prediction.

The order of presentation of the three relation-changing communications was randomized within each group. Directly after reading each communication the subject was required to evaluate it on three separate five-point scales in respect to how much the communication pleased him, how much it persuaded him, and how accurate it appeared to him. A composite index was computed by summing the three ratings.

Results

Table 12 displays the mean ratings by the three groups of each of the three communications on each of the three scales and on the composite index. Each single scale ranges from 0 to 5, the composite from 0 to 15. Each 3×3 table is arranged so that the communications predicted to have the greatest appeal lie along the main diagonal.

TABLE 12. *Responses to the countercommunications; mean ratings for three structure groups, Study 1*

Rating scale	Group	N	AS	COUNTER * FA	FS
Pleased	1	22	4.23	3.50	2.18
	2	32	2.69	3.78	2.28
	3	28	2.21	3.18	3.89
Persuaded	1	22	3.27	2.59	2.14
	2	32	2.25	3.06	2.41
	3	28	2.25	2.75	3.71
Accurate	1	22	3.68	3.45	3.05
	2	32	3.00	3.41	2.97
	3	28	2.93	3.36	3.89
Composite	1	22	11.18	9.54	7.37
	2	32	7.94	10.25	7.66
	3	28	7.39	9.29	11.49

* AS denotes the communication arguing that art will help sales; FA, that Fenwick will decide against art; FS, that Fenwick has been poor for sales.

Casual inspection of Table 12 suggests confirmation of the hypothesis with regard to both the primary and secondary predictions derived from it. To assess statistical significance, four analyses of variance were carried out. Of these, we present in detail only the analysis of the composite ratings. (The analyses of the single scales all come out with the same set of conclusions as the composite analysis.)

The general form of the design is that which Lindquist (1953) calls a "Type I Design." However, the usual mode of analysis of such designs was refined to handle the particular hypothesis of our study.

To test the primary prediction that subjects will be more receptive to balance-producing communications than to all others, the following "comparison" (Cochran and Cox, 1950) was formed:

	AS	FA	FS
1.	+2	−1	−1
2.	−1	+2	−1
3.	−1	−1	+2

This comparison is a component of the interaction between groups and communications.

To test the secondary prediction that subjects will be differentially receptive to communications which imply the fewest further cognitive changes to produce total balance, we form the comparison:

	AS	FA	FS
1.	0	+1	−1
2.	0	0	0
3.	−1	+1	0

Since this comparison is partially confounded with between-communication effects, a separate between-communications sum of squares is not extracted. Instead, a 4 d.f. "residual between-cell effects" sum of squares is formed. The sum of squares for the two hypotheses and for the residual between-cell sum of squares are all tested against the within-subject error term. The analysis displayed in Table 13 shows that both predictions are very strongly confirmed. Furthermore, the insignificant residual implies that there are no systematic effects in the data other than those specified by the hypotheses. This undercuts the possibility that the secondary prediction might have been "artifactually" confirmed because of the greater intrinsic appeal of the Fenwick-Art communication.

TABLE 13. *Analysis of variance, Study 1*

Source	df	Mean square	F	p
Between groups	2	16.70	2.80	<.10
Subjects in groups	79	5.96	—	—
Major prediction	1	415.03	62.22	<.001
Secondary prediction	1	103.07	15.45	<.001
Residual between cell	4	3.23	<1.00	Not sig.
Error within subjects	158	6.67	—	—

The general conclusion that seems to be required is that the hypothesis given above is strongly confirmed; that imbalance reduction within a structure of attitudinal cognitions will tend to follow a least effortful path. If only a single sign change is required, the receptivity to a communication advocating that change is relatively great. As between those communications implying two sign changes vs. those implying three, there is somewhat less difference, though the least-effort principle is still strongly supported.

However, one possible objection to be considered at this point would note that the more effortful approaches to balancing these structures involve changing evaluations of concepts as well as of relations. Since the change communications are concerned directly only with the three relations between concepts, the subjects may have felt more hesitant at the prospect of changing their direct evaluations of the concepts than would have otherwise been the case. To this line of argument it may be countered that the subjects were specifically instructed to feel free to change both concept evaluations and perceived relations as they thought through the import of the communications.

Nevertheless these considerations point to an important limitation in the data: from them we know little about what happens *after* the "least effortful" countercommunication is accepted; or, to put it another way, we do not know whether the making of a change that promises balance restoration actually and always leads to attainment of final balance. The major purpose of our second study was simply to follow the subjects through the full sequence in which an unbalanced structure is established, potentially imbalance-reducing communications are received, and changes over the whole structure are made and stabilized.

STUDY 2

Our preliminary hypothesis was that initial differences in the structure of attitudinal cognitions would be related to differences in the extent and type of final formal balance achieved by the subjects.

Method

In this study three groups of undergraduate subjects were assigned to "role-play" the same three cognitive structures used in the previous study. The actual communications used in establishing these structures were similar to, but not identical with, those used in the first study. Three additional groups, to be explained below, were also run. The total number of original subjects was 119, of whom 72 were retained in the final analysis.[1] The major difference between this study and

1. As in the previous experiment, immediately after reading the role-playing (structure-establishing) communications, all subjects were tested on scales dealing with their feelings toward the three concepts and their beliefs

the previous one is that it enabled adequate measurement not only of the subjects' responses to the three countercommunications but it also allowed for observation of changes in cognitive structure after the subject had expressed his direct evaluations of the countercommunications. This was made possible by administering an instrument containing six rating scales at *two points* during the experimental sequence: the first administration came immediately after the subject had read the material designed to establish the assigned structure; the second came after he had completed his evaluations of the countercommunications. The instrument used contained separate rating scales eliciting evaluations of the three concepts, "high sales volume," "modern art," and "Fenwick" and of the three relations between these concepts when taken two at a time. The scores varied over a range of eleven points from extreme positive to extreme negative. Differences in evaluation occurring from the first to the second administration of the instrument could be taken as evidence of change within the indicated portion of the total structure. Thus, for each structure group it could be asked: What kind of structure do the members of the group typically achieve after evaluating and thinking through the countercommunications?

Results

A replicative check on the major findings obtained in the previous study can be made by examining the subjects' evaluative responses to the three countercommunications. As in the previous study, after receiving the structure-establishing communications and after reproducing the assigned structure, each subject received, in random order, the three separate

----

about the relationships between them. Again, only those subjects were retained who succeeded in reproducing the structures on which they had been trained. Of the 47 rejected subjects, 19 had distorted the assigned structure so as to achieve "premature balance."

countercommunications. Thus one of these (AS) presented arguments to the effect that the relation between displaying modern art and sales volume is really positive, while the other two countercommunications (FA and FS) asserted negative relationships between the concepts (i.e. "Fenwick really will be prevented from displaying modern art." [2] "Fenwick's sales record is really a very bad one").

TABLE 14. *Responses to the countercommunications; mean ratings for three structure groups, Study 2*

Rating scale	Group	N	AS	COUNTER FA	FS
Pleased	1	13	4.62	2.85	2.00
	2	11	2.18	3.45	2.82
	3	11	2.18	3.82	3.91
Persuaded	1	13	3.15	2.08	2.54
	2	11	2.09	3.45	2.91
	3	11	1.82	3.73	3.91
Accurate	1	13	3.54	3.15	3.15
	2	11	2.45	3.82	3.18
	3	11	2.45	4.09	3.82
Composite	1	13	11.31	8.08	7.69
	2	11	6.73	10.73	8.91
	3	11	6.45	11.64	11.64

As Table 14 reveals, groups 1, 2, and 3 in this study show substantially the same pattern of response to the counter-communications as their counterparts in the first study. However, a few irregularities appear. The major one is that in group 3 the countercommunication asserting that Fenwick

2. It should be noted that this countercommunication differs from the FA countercommunication used in the first study, which offered evidence supporting the assertion that "Fenwick really does not plan to set up a modern art display"; the FA countercommunication used in the present study offered evidence in support of the assertion that "Fenwick will be prevented (by the objections and recalcitrance of his employees) from displaying modern art."

will be prevented from hanging the art display is rated just as high as the countercommunication asserting that Fenwick has a bad sales record.

The analysis of variance of the composite index, given in Table 15, suggests the following conclusions: (1) the major prediction is again quite strongly borne out; (2) the secondary prediction is supported as strongly as in the first study; (3) the significance of the residual forces us to take seriously the irregularities in Table 14, particularly the very high rating of the FA countercommunication in group 3. Differences between the first and second studies in the actual wording of the structure-establishing communications and countercommunications may account for the discrepancy. Incidentally, further analysis indicates that the secondary hypothesis cannot be written off as an artifact of a strong FA countercommunication.

TABLE 15. *Analysis of variance, Study 2*

Source	df	Mean square	F	p
Between groups	2	11.65	1.92	Not sig.
Subjects in groups	32	6.08	—	—
Major prediction	1	205.48	26.57	<.001
Secondary prediction	1	92.75	11.99	<.001
Residual between cell	4	22.36	2.89	<.05
Error within subjects	64	7.73	—	—

The additional three groups (1', 2', and 3') were trained, exposed, and tested on the same materials except for one variation. With these three groups the single unbalanced relation in each of the three structures was more strongly established than in groups 1, 2, and 3. This was achieved by supporting that relation with more extreme and extensive evidence. Scale measures taken immediately after exposure to these materials indicate that "stronger establishment" was indeed achieved. Behind this variation was an interest in whether the least effortful (one sign change) path to balance could be blocked off, thus leading to greater use of two- and three-sign-change resolutions. Figure 3 depicts the initial structures of groups 1', 2', and 3'.

Figure 3. The Three Additional Structures

Structure 1'   *Structure 2'*   *Structure 3'*

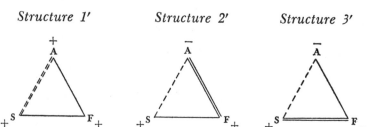

As in Fig. 2, a solid line represents a positive relation, a dotted line represents a negative relation. Double lines indicate very strongly established relations.

Table 16 gives the mean communication ratings for these additional groups, and Table 17, the analysis of variance of the composite index. The last three mean squares of Table 17 are strikingly similar to the comparable quantities in Table 15. The difference between the two sets of three groups in communication effects is in the strength with which the major prediction is confirmed. Groups 1', 2', and 3' manifest less preference for the separate communications which, if accepted, would restore their respective structures to balance than do groups 1, 2, and 3. This can be observed directly from Table 16, wherein the diagonal entries are far less prominent than in Table 14. (A significance test for this specific effect can be constructed by pooling the differences in corresponding diagonals and testing against an error term based on the mean squares attributable to subjects in groups. The effect is significant at the .05 level.)

The lesser magnitude of the major effect is, of course, to be expected, because the initially unbalanced bands were established more strongly and were thereby less easily assailable by the countercommunications. That the major hypothesis is confirmed at all seems to testify to the strength of the average subject's preference for a "one-change" route toward balance. Thus subjects who "needed" a certain communication (to balance their structures through a single sign change) were

TABLE 16. *Responses to the countercommunications; mean ratings for the extra three structure groups, Study 2*

Rating scale	Group	N	AS	COUNTER FA	FS
Pleased	1′	13	4.15	2.62	2.59
	2′	13	2.69	3.15	2.69
	3′	11	1.82	3.82	3.00
Persuaded	1′	13	2.85	2.31	2.69
	2′	13	2.00	2.69	2.69
	3′	11	1.27	3.45	3.45
Accurate	1′	13	3.15	3.46	3.23
	2′	13	2.77	3.15	3.23
	3′	11	2.27	3.82	3.73
Composite	1′	13	10.15	8.38	8.46
	2′	13	7.46	9.00	8.62
	3′	11	5.36	11.09	10.18

in general more receptive to it than those who did not need it (i.e. those for whom it did not offer a balanced resolution); this was so *in spite of the fact that for the former subjects the communication was more in disagreement with the initially established band than for the latter subjects.*

Two things remain to be noted with respect to Tables 16 and 17. First, we observe that the unexpectedly high receptivity of group 3 to the FA communication is replicated in group 3'. Second, we must acknowledge that the basic purpose for the construction of groups 1', 2', and 3' is not achieved; the attractiveness of the communications permitting a one-sign change toward balance is diminished somewhat, but the attractiveness of the other communications is not thereby enhanced. *Apparently it is difficult to elicit a strongly positive immediate reaction to communications which merely pave the way toward ultimate balance, instead of providing balancing material immediately.*

TABLE 17. *Analysis of variance, extra groups, Study 2*

Source	df	Mean square	F	p
Between groups	2	4.47	<1.00	Not sig.
Subjects in groups	34	7.96	—	—
Major prediction	1	58.77	8.45	<.01
Secondary prediction	1	95.09	13.67	<.001
Residual between cell	4	24.31	3.49	<.05
Error within subjects	68	6.96	—	—

While the data so far reviewed confirm and add to the findings of the first experiment it cannot be definitely asserted that high evaluation of the persuasive force of a countercommunication will necessarily be followed by cognitive changes that are totally consistent with that countercommunication. Whether or not subjects who accept a given communication that is potentially balance-restoring then go on to balance in the expected way is, it will be remembered, the very question to which our second study was mainly addressed.

The most direct approach to this question is to ask whether the groups differ from each other in the frequency and form of balanced structures achieved after exposure to the countercommunications. This can be determined from the data collected in the second administration of the set of rating scales concerned with the three concepts and the relations between them. Examining the signs (positive or negative) of the subjects' ratings of the three concepts and their three relationships, it is found that only among those subjects assigned to groups 1 and 1' is there an impressive number of subjects who achieved final balance over the whole structure. Of the 26 subjects in these two groups 16 achieved completely balanced final structures. All but one of these subjects ended with a structure returned to balance by following through on the implications of the countercommunication most popular with this group; i.e. they changed their evaluation of the relationship between modern art and sales volume from negative to positive and thus achieved the totally consistent pattern of beliefs in which a liked person, Fenwick, who has a good sales record, will display liked modern art, which will foster the positive goal of increasing sales volume.

TABLE 18. *Frequency of attainment of balance, Study 2*

Groups	N	NUMBER ATTAINING BALANCE-TYPE:			
		3 plus *	*2 plus* *	*1 plus* *	*No balance*
1 and 1'	26	15	1	0	10
2 and 2'	24	4	1	1	18
3 and 3'	22	0	1	3	18

* In the "3 plus" balanced resolution, all concepts have positive sign; in the "2 plus" resolution, sales and Fenwick are plus, art minus; in the "1 plus" resolution, only sales is plus, with art and Fenwick minus.

The three forms of balance are arranged to correspond with the communications in Table 16. "Appropriate" balance-types lie along the diagonal of the 3 x 3 table.

This same final structure is achieved by four of the twenty-four subjects (groups 2 and 2') assigned to the second cognitive structure (in which the discrepant belief is the one that asserts that liked Fenwick will display disliked modern art). Only one subject attained the form of total balance presumably appropriate for these groups, namely that liked Fenwick, with the good sales record, will be prevented from displaying disliked modern art, which would damage sales. One other subject attained a third type of balance, and eighteen subjects did not attain a balanced structure.

In groups 3 and 3', three subjects attained the appropriate balance, one subject an inappropriate balance, and eighteen reached no balance. Table 18 summarizes these frequencies.

The fact that so many of the subjects did not achieve final structural balance should not be taken to mean that they did not alter the sets of beliefs and evaluations with which they began. To the contrary all subjects substantially changed one or more ratings of concepts and relations between them, and most gave evidence of having altered their evaluations and beliefs in ways which somehow yielded varying degrees of satisfaction. From these facts, it seems to us to be apparent that the assumption that persons holding unbalanced cognitive structures are motivated to return these to "balance," while not disconfirmed, was shown to be part of a more complex story.

TABLE 19. *Changes in concept evaluations and relation signs; magnitude and direction of mean before-after change*

		CONCEPTS			RELATIONS		
Group	N	Sales	Art	Fenwick	AS	FA	FS
1	13	−.15	−.23	−1.39	4.16	−2.62	−3.00
2	11	.00	3.37	−1.91	5.45	−4.18	−3.54
3	11	.18	2.27	.18	3.81	−5.18	−4.18
1'	13	−.08	−.08	−.93	3.38	−2.39	−2.92
2'	13	.00	2.46	−1.38	3.54	−2.46	−3.16
3'	11	−.18	.63	.91	1.81	−4.37	−4.00

Table 19 presents the before-after changes in group mean ratings of each of the three concepts and three relations. Since each of the six scales had a maximum range of 11 points, a change of 5.5 would necessarily imply a crossing of the neutral point of the scale, i.e. a change in sign after receipt of the countercommunications. However, since initial ratings were generally not at the absolute extremes, a change of 4.0 is approximately sufficient to reverse any given sign.

Table 19 shows that all of the relations change in the directions advocated by the respective communications. The changes are large enough to make it unlikely that they are artifacts of repeated measurement; rather it would seem that subjects in all groups are by and large somewhat influenced by all three communications. Further, and more to the point, the patterns of mean changes in the last three columns of Table 19 display considerable irregularity from what one would expect on the basis of tendencies making for attainment of structural balance as we have formally defined it up to this point. (Analyses of variance in the fashion of those in Tables 15 and 17 reveal no significant effects consistent with formal balance.)

The failure of the subjects, particularly in groups 2, 2′, 3, and 3′, to achieve such balance in their cognitive structures has already been presaged in Table 18. Table 19 gives clues to the nature of the failure. In groups 2 and 2′, there is a disproportionately large change on the Art-Sales relation, as well as a tendency to change the negative evaluation of modern art toward a positive evaluation. In groups 3 and 3′, the biggest change is on the Fenwick-Art relation (this change is coordinate with the unexpectedly favorable receptivity to the Fenwick-Art countercommunication, cf. Tables 14 and 16).

These irregularities suggest that, in addition to a force propelling the individual toward the redress of imbalance as heretofore defined, another major force may be operative. *This second force is conceived as driving the individual toward the maximization of potential gain and the minimiza-*

tion of potential loss. By "gain" and "loss" in the context of the present materials we mean the gain or loss of *sales,* the dominant value for the store owner. In general, by "gain" or "loss" we mean the fulfillment or frustration of motives *other* than those driving the individual toward formal cognitive balance. (However, the possibility of representing other motive forces in an expanded conceptualization of cognitive balance is examined in a later section.)

To clarify these considerations let us examine the situations faced by subjects in structure groups 2 and 3, respectively. If structure 2 is balanced by the most economical path, the resulting pattern of beliefs does not promise any further gain in sales but merely the elimination of the threat of a potential loss of sales. By accepting the belief that Fenwick will, after all, be prevented from going ahead with his plan for a modern art display, a structure is achieved in which a good department manager, Fenwick, will desist from doing something that would have decreased sales volume. At best all that is promised is a retention of the status quo. But the communication arguing that modern art displays really *increase* sales avails the subject of a more "gainful" resolution: perhaps the art display will help after all. The subjects of structure 2, while not immediately impressed by the Art-Sales countercommunication (Tables 14 and 16), do ultimately tend to register this change in belief.

From the point of view of potential gain and loss the members of the third structure group face a severely unpleasant situation. In this structure formal balance can be achieved merely by accepting and interiorizing the judgment that Fenwick has really done a poor job all along. The resulting balanced structure would be to the effect that disliked Fenwick has really done a poor job and is now going to carry through a distasteful plan which will injure sales volume. Here we have a totally balanced state of affairs which at the same time is clearly unsatisfying. Whereas the reorganization of the first structure along the lines of formal balance promises new gains and that of the second structure promises avoidance of loss, that of the third structure confirms the expectation that the worst that was feared will come to pass. Indeed, it asserts a consistency between injury and its negative source. Therefore it is not surprising that subjects in structure 3 are receptive to, and moved by, the communication suggesting that Fenwick will be prevented from displaying modern art. In accepting this communication they are expressing an aspiration that "the evil hand will be stayed from the evil deed."

One might wonder why subjects in groups 3 and 3' are not more substantially moved to see modern art as potentially helpful to sales, since that is the gainful belief. The plausible answer is that this belief is too unbalanced, too discordant, with the concept evaluations these subjects have initially been given: the art display is an unpleasant idea conceived by someone they dislike, and therefore not likely to be seen as potentially helpful.

Emerging from this discussion then is the following general proposition: *In resolving cognitive discrepancies of the sort represented by our materials, subjects seek not only the attainment of cognitive balance and consistency but they seek also to alter their beliefs and evaluations in ways that will maximize expected gain and minimize expected loss; when both forces converge so that they may be gratified through the same change or changes a formally "balanced" outcome will be achieved; when these forces diverge the typical outcome will not meet the requirements of a simple formal definition of cognitive balance.*

IMPLICATIONS

The dual-force conception

In interpreting some of the results of our second study we arrived at a dual-force conception of the dynamics of cognitive balancing. Similar dual-force conceptions in related areas can be construed from the writings of at least three other theorists. Deutsch and Solomon (1959) have reported that where incompetent performance is criticized by one's peers, there is both a force toward balance (whereby one would accept the criticism) and a force toward "positivity" (whereby one would resent the criticism). In Festinger's (1954) "theory of social comparison," it is asserted that people are motivated to locate themselves in social groups with opinions and abilities comparable to their own (a kind of homeostatic tendency), but that in addition there is an upward push toward the possession of qualities *superior* to those of the comparison group (a self-satisfaction tendency). Harary (1959), in listing the forces thought to be most generally operative in sociometric groupings, specifies a balance tendency (people tend to like their friends' friends and their enemies' enemies, etc.) and a positivity tendency (other things being equal, liking predominates over disliking).

However, despite our similar effort to delineate a distinction between balance and "other forms of gain" we do not contend that these forces constitute a true bipolarity. In fact, if we draw upon Heider's "unit relation" concept, the force toward "other forms of gain" may be viewed simply as a special case of the balance force, endowed with unique properties. Thus the situation in which the self experiences, or is implicated in, a motive-frustrating state of affairs may be formalized as an unbalanced $(-p+)$ band, with a unit relation connecting the self and that state of affairs: i.e. "Bad consequences (—) will accrue to (p) me (+)." Other frustrating situations are similarly formalizable as imbalances:

I (+) failed to get (n) what I wanted (+).
I (+) did (p) something reprehensible (—).
I (+) am engaged in (p) an unrewarding job (—).

These special types of situation often form the basis for experiments on Festinger's (1957) dissonance theory. They constitute an interesting class of cases, since they present a pithy array of the gamut of human "losses," e.g. pain, frustration, guilt, shame, boredom. It has not yet been established that these "hedonic imbalances" obey the same laws of resolution as other imbalances. Nevertheless, such a theoretical position seems eminently defensible.

It is on this basis that we have contended that the ostensibly "unbalanced" outcomes obtained in our second experiment from subjects in groups 2, 2′, 3, and 3′ are in the main due to a striving toward the reduction of just such implicit hedonic imbalances as are described above. Thus we have pointed out that a common final pattern of cognitions in groups 2 and 2′ consists of a seemingly unbalanced set of beliefs that "liked Fenwick who has an effective sales record will display disliked modern art which will nevertheless have a positive effect upon sales volume"; but when the hedonic purport of this structure is reduced to a single implied cognition the result is a (+p+) band, i.e. "a good consequence (high sales volume) will accrue to me." The typical final structure attained in groups 3 and 3′ is, on the same basis, reducible to (—n+), i.e. "a bad consequence (reduction of sales volume) will be prevented from accruing to me."

We suggest then that the acceptability of a structure that, in formal terms, is unbalanced may depend largely on whether the single hedonic band to which it is reducible is, in itself, balanced or unbalanced. A great deal of further work is needed to clarify how persons may deal in a *unified* way with situations (such as those in the present studies) involving the two classes of imbalance, if indeed such unified treatment is feasible. Systematic pursuit of this problem will probably contribute greater power to the available group of cognitive balance theories.

A microprocess analysis of cognitive balancing

Despite our finding that the striving toward formal cognitive balance may be countermanded by a striving toward other forms of gain, the implication that the latter may be reduced to the former suggests that the balance principle is one of high generality. As such it deserves still closer examination.

Following the lead of other theorists we have treated the striving toward cognitive balance in terms of gross changes in the signs of concepts and their relations to one another. Yet it seems clear that when a subject changes his evaluation of modern art from positive to negative, or the believed relation between modern art and sales volume from negative to positive, such changes must have a background in some mediating process or set of processes.

One probable route toward an understanding of these processes is opened by designating the kinds of sign changes with which we have been so far concerned as relatively *molar* changes. An examination of the kinds of changes that may underlie them, a "microprocess" analysis in conjectural terms, is the main intent of this section.

The necessity for such a shift in level of analysis is made clear by certain considerations that arise in answer to the following question: If cognitive imbalance is motivating and if it can be eliminated by a few simple sign changes within a structure, why do not subjects universally and simply make the necessary changes whenever they encounter imbalance?

If no effort, or even if only slight effort, were required they could and presumably always would redress unbalanced beliefs. But our findings and those of other researchers indicate that balance-seeking (even when redefined to include the kinds of implicitly balanced hedonic outcomes discussed above), though a significant determinant of cognitive operations, does not always eventuate in balance-attainment. *Clearly, forces opposing balance-producing changes must be present.* A microprocess analysis will expose the complex interplay between the balance tendency and the forces preventing the attainment of balance.

In what follows, we make working theoretical assumptions in order to clarify the issues at stake. Alternative assumptions could readily be made at various points; but at present there is not nearly enough evidence to resolve conflicting assumptions. A particular position is asserted in the interest of coherent presentation.

Our first assumption is that any imbalance of the kind we have been concerned with can be analyzed as one or more ambivalences. Thus in exploring the mechanics of imbalance-reduction, we need concern ourselves only with microprocesses that serve to reduce ambivalence; these microprocesses will serve also to reduce imbalance. By ambivalence we mean the simultaneous presence of positive and negative affect in reaction to a cognized object. This definition is meant to be considerably milder than that in the corresponding psychoanalytic usage; we include instances where the affect is slight or where it is transient.

This focus on ambivalence is inspired by considerations raised by the valuable contribution of Osgood and Tannenbaum (1955); see also Osgood, Suci, and Tannenbaum (1958). These investigators experimentally created "incongruities" between cognitive concepts by, for example, associating liked persons with disliked objects. Their "principle of congruity" when brought to bear upon the results predicts that the evaluations of the person and the object will regress in the direction of a common value: the liked person when associated with the disliked object becomes less liked while the object becomes less disliked. This principle is by and large well borne out by their experimental data.

Osgood and Tannenbaum suggest a mathematical form for describing such a process, but that need not concern us here. Instead we raise the question of whether their basic hypothesis is widely applicable; whether the incongruous coupling of two affectively significant objects will *usually* produce regression of the two affects toward zero.

The Osgood and Tannenbaum principle suggests a set of metaphors which will prove convenient as we address ourselves to this question. We shall refer to affect as "charge" (with a sign and magnitude) and to a relation between concepts as a connection which causes the "induction" of charge from one concept onto another.

To introduce our alternative formulation let us consider the state of affairs when an asserted positive connection between a positive concept and a negative concept is first perceived by the subject. The induction of negative charge onto the positive concept produces some degree of ambivalence. Similarly the induction of positive charge onto the negative concept produces ambivalence. These ambivalences are *tension-arousing;* they set in motion processes directed toward their removal. If the ambivalences are not removed, they continue to be unpleasant, even painful, to the subject so long as he continues to think about the concepts at issue. A resolution of these ambivalences based solely on the mutual "running down" of the charges would probably prove to be an inefficient one. Osgood and Tannenbaum's data suggest that it would take a long time for the equilibrium state of equal charges to be reached (even with concepts of weak affect). Thus in order to reach this state, the individual must suffer the presence of ambivalences over a long period. More efficient resolutions of ambivalence (imbalance), if available to the subject and if applicable to the situation, would be likely to take priority.

There is one other basis for contending that the running down of affective charges may be a comparatively inefficient way of reducing ambivalences. Let us consider the following hypothetical case: Suppose that a moderately positive concept, via connection with a highly negative concept, were to have its charge run down across the neutral point and become negative. This originally positive concept presumably possessed predominantly positive relations with other positive concepts (and negative relations with negative concepts). For it now to become negative would create new imbalances (ambivalences), should the attention of the subject be directed to these other relations.

In the light of these considerations we suggest that the process postulated by Osgood and Tannenbaum is not necessarily uniquely operative during the full aftermath of an encounter with an incongruous relation between two affectively significant concepts. We suggest that, instead, the running-down process is the *first one* invoked whenever incongruity (i.e. cognitive imbalance) is encountered; but when the affect associated with either concept has undergone some initial shift the potential creation of new imbalances produces considerable disorder in the person's cognitive system: a threat of further imbalance (on other bands) is posed. Protection from this threat may be provided by mechanisms which forestall the occurrence of prolonged ambivalence. We have already suggested that such mechanisms are often available and applicable.[3]

3. In a paper (1960) published as this volume goes to press, Osgood, in reviewing theories of cognitive consistency, acknowledges and discusses several such mechanisms.

In presenting our speculative elucidation of some of these mechanisms we adopt the following terminology: When concept A induces charge onto concept B such as to create ambivalence on concept B, we refer to element B as the "threatened concept," to concept A as the "intrusive concept," and to the relation between A and B as the "intrusive relation." (A few other metaphorical usages will be defined in the appropriate context.)

The list of these mechanisms would include: (1) altering the intrusive relation; (2) altering the charge on the intrusive concept; (3) isolating a subpart of the threatened concept from the remainder of the concept; (4) counteracting the intrusive charge by bolstering the threatened concept with a "reassuring" charge. We suggest that these are four "microprocesses" involved in the achievement of those "molar" sign changes by which unbalanced cognitive bands are restored to balance.

In Abelson's (1959) analysis of modes of resolution of belief dilemmas, the first two of the above processes are called "denial," the third "differentiation," and the fourth "bolstering." The second and third processes, however, are quite similar, as we shall see.

Considerable explication of these processes is called for. In particular, we must specify them in a nonarbitrary way. The individual cannot "neutralize," "counteract," etc. at will, but must operate within a set of constraints. Consider the imbalance paraphrased from one of our experimental conditions: "Fenwick (whom I like a great deal) proposes to display modern art (which irritates me)." This unbalanced band $(+p-)$ simultaneously creates two ambivalences: (1) Fenwick, possessed of good personal qualities, has committed himself to a foolish activity which reflects badly upon his personal qualities; (2) Modern art, possessed of bad qualities, has found a supporter in good friend Fenwick, implying that modern art has good qualities after all. The distress of the former might be expressed by "What's gotten into him?"; of the latter by "What can there be in it?" Which of these two distresses would guide further cognitive operations is likely to be determined by the comparative magnitudes of the signs of the two objects. One might assume that the concept with the stronger sign will be protected against the intrusive, ambivalence-creating influence of the weaker sign. However, it turns out that this assumption is not critical because processes that successfully protect one concept also protect the other.

Process 1: altering the intrusive relation. Let us proceed from the point of view of the first question, "What's gotten into him?" Modern art is the "intrusive" concept and Fenwick the "threatened" concept. Process 1 would require denial of the intrusive relation; that is, some assertion of the form, "He does not propose to display modern art." This assertion cannot readily be made without some support, for it can too easily be refuted by subsequent events. A strong reality component is involved. Support might be found in two ways; by disclaimers, i.e. reasons why the relation should be considered false ("There has been malicious office gossip about Fenwick lately") and/or by direct assertion of the opposite ("He distinctly told me himself that he despises modern art"). There may well be dynamic differences between these two types of support, but what they have in common is an appeal to new information, to *additional or alternative relations* which make possible the denial of the unbalancing intrusive relation.

If the present example occurred in real life such alternative relations might be discovered when and if the store owner talks to Fenwick. Barring this, the store owner may try to avail himself of assertions which nullify the Fenwick-Art relation; the success of such an attempt depends on the *availability* of strong disclaimers or counterassertions. The function of the balance-producing countercommunications used in our experiments is to make such material available.

Rosenberg's affect-reversal experiments reported in Chapter 2 show quite clearly that cognitive materials may be readily available by which alternative, balance-restoring relations can be discovered and brought into use. When his subjects undergo sizable affect change toward some concept such as "foreign aid" they experience imbalance on each separate band relating foreign aid to some other affectively significant (i.e. charge-bearing) concept; one of the prominent balance-restoring mechanisms employed by these subjects is the alteration of the believed relationships between those concepts and the central concept "foreign aid." Content analysis of their "think out loud" records shows that one of the main methods (though not the only one) through which this is accomplished is by searching out additional or alternative relations by which the original relation is displaced.

Process 2: neutralizing the charge on the intrusive concept. This process has to do not with the relation carrying the intrusive charge, but with the concept giving rise to the intrusion. The threatened concept must be "insulated" from the *charge* of the intrusive concept. Here again we must spell this out in a nonarbitrary way.

For this process to occur, there must be some cognitive materials available which when invoked make possible the assertion of a sign opposite to the original sign of the intrusive concept. To understand how such an assertion of the opposite sign is possible, it must be recognized that a cognitive concept is usually not homogeneous but contains subparts by which it is denoted; furthermore, it frequently lies within a nexus of relations with other concepts, which are thereby connoted by it.

In the specific example at hand, modern art is disliked, but probably not completely so and in every detail. It has some good characteristics which may be made more salient. Also it may already be believed that it is instrumental to some positive values and may be supported by persons or groups who are esteemed; the relations underlying these connotations may be strengthened while opposite relations may be weakened.

Thus, continuing our illustration of this process, the store owner may come up with the notion that modern art, though meaningless and possibly fraudulent, is after all, sometimes colorful. The advantage in recalling and reconstructing this positive attribute of modern art is that Fenwick can now be seen as associated with this positive attribute, rather than with the negative totality, "modern art." Thus, "What Fenwick is really interested in is a *colorful* display." The offensive band now becomes (+p+) instead of (+p−). What happens to the negative sign on modern art? Presumably it has become detached from connection with Fenwick. The sign attaching to the totality, "modern art," is conserved; it is merely redistributed among the subparts of the object. The "meaning" of modern art in the context "Fenwick is going to display it" is based upon a set of subparts different from its meaning in other contexts and differing correspondingly in the affective sign it carries. This phenomenon is what Asch (1940) has referred to as "change in the object of judgment" as distinguished from change in the "judgment of the object."

Process 3: isolating a subpart of the threatened concept. This process involves isolating the subpart of the concept receiving the intrusive charge from the remainder of the concept and is thus parallel to process 2. In the Fenwick-modern art example, it might take some form such as the following: "Fenwick does have a number of peculiar enthusiasms; this probably accounts for his interest in modern art. There is no accounting for tastes." Here a negative subpart of Fenwick is selected for linkage with the intrusive negative concept and the resulting band (−p−) is isolated so that the over-all sign of the Fenwick concept remains unchallenged.

For processes 2 and 3, one may question how it is that the

subpart selected for attachment to the intrusive relation can be insulated from the remainder of the concept, which is opposite in sign. If ambivalence is the heart of imbalance, then the existence, much less the bringing into prominence, of a subpart with the "wrong" sign implies further imbalance rather than less. To avoid this further imbalance it is necessary for a "barrier" to be imposed between the subpart and the remainder of the concept. It is possible to conceptualize the natural unity between a concept and one of its subparts as a "band" composed of the positive concept, the negative subpart, and a positive relation between them $(+p-)$. The imposition of a barrier means neutralizing the positive relation. The two modes of process 1 would presumably apply here: i.e. this positive relation may be disclaimed and/or its opposite may be asserted.

The store owner's process 3 resolution quoted above illustrates a disclaimer: "There is no accounting for tastes." The function of this disclaimer is to render false the implicit relationship between whole and subpart; thus it is implied that it is not true that a man's tastes are an essential part of him.

Assertion of the opposite might take the form, "In my contacts with him he has been sober and sensible; this art thing is another side of him entirely, quite different from the side that I see."

A similar kind of operation is required for process 2. Thus when the store owner says that modern art is colorful, he makes it necessary to assert also that colorfulness is not what he typically thinks of when he thinks of modern art; or he may even make some stronger assertion, e.g. that colorfulness is quite distinct from and has nothing to do with other aspects of modern art, such as its meaninglessness.

Process 4: bolstering the threatened concept with a "reassuring" charge. This way of counteracting the intrusive charge does not really resolve the imbalance. Rather, it protects against the running down of a concept sign by restoring some of the affect that has been lost. This process may be used in conjunction with processes 1, 2, or 3. The exemplifications of processes 2 and 3 given above contain overtones of this additional process; after detachment of subparts it is possible to reassert and reinforce contentions to the effect that Fenwick is indeed sober and sensible, or that modern art is indeed meaningless.

Underlying operations. Though we have distinguished four separate processes assumed to underlie cognitive balancing, further analysis suggests that common to each of them are certain basic cognitive operations. The key operation might be called "selective search," by which is meant the attempt by the individual to locate attributes of objects and to locate relations between objects such that the balance-seeking processes are appropriately served. It is a necessary and systematic assumption that such selective search involves a "scanning" of "files" containing denotative and connotative characterizations of objects; these characterizations have been learned through previous encounters with these objects or with communications or thoughts about them.

Conditions under which the microprocesses are employed

For purposes of exposition we have so far spoken of the "microprocesses" as the underlying mediational events leading to sign changes which restore unbalanced cognitions to balance. However, a major restriction on the generality of our analysis should be noted. While the first of the four processes we have described ("altering the intrusive relation") may be operative in any situation in which two affectively charged concepts are linked in an unbalanced way, this does not seem to be the case for the remaining three.

As we have described them each of these three processes,

if successfully employed, produces change in the affective sign of a concept by altering that concept's phenomenal content: some subpart or number of subparts is singled out as more salient than it previously was; some other subpart or number of subparts is eliminated from the concept or is rendered less central to that concept. To characterize this situation we invoke once again Asch's (1940) contention that in the attitude-change situation what really changes is the "object of judgment." Our second, third, and fourth processes refer to situations in which this is the case. Unlike Asch, however, we do not assume that this is the only possible case; rather we assume that there are many situations in which the affective sign of a concept will undergo change while the denotative content of that concept remains quite stable. We refer then to situations in which intrusive charge is induced onto such a concept from some other concept and the sign of the former is *directly* altered; i.e. our postulated microprocesses 2, 3, and 4 do not intervene.

We suggest that this latter case is most likely to occur when the original affective charge of the concept onto which opposite charge is being induced is of quite low magnitude in comparison to the magnitude of the induced charge. In such a situation the induction of stronger and opposite affective charge will create little or no ambivalence; direct alteration of the affective response toward the concept will not be opposed by competing affective responses. It seems to us that many of the attitude-change phenomena produced in both experimental and nonexperimental settings are of this variety.

One further restriction upon our analysis of microprocesses needs to be elaborated. We do not maintain that whenever imbalances involving sizable ambivalence are encountered the person will always and dependably resolve them through processes such as the ones we have postulated. The *outcome* of an attempt to achieve balance is greatly dependent upon the contents of the cognitive "files"; i.e. the material available with which to implement the four processes. The history of the individual's dealings with the attitude object (and with other objects in the same area) is clearly of crucial importance.

Indeed we are now in a position to formulate a schematic answer to the question with which this section began: Why do not subjects universally and simply make the necessary sign changes when they encounter inconsistency?

A simple but compelling answer seems to be that for all individuals in some cognitive areas (and possibly for some individuals in nearly all cognitive areas) there is not available a file of learned distinctions, categories, relations, etc. with which the microprocesses we have described can be employed toward a successful conclusion. Even where such a process is undertaken it may lead the person to a point where the promised balance is outweighed by its cost in further imbalance. As illustration we may point again to the situation encountered in processes 2 and 3 when by highlighting an opposite-signed subpart of a concept there is produced imbalance *within* that concept. The resolution of this imbalance by the imposing of a barrier between the subpart and its reference concept may be impossible by virtue of a lack of the necessary file material; or it may be impossible by virtue of a general characteristic of "conceptual inflexibility" or because the natural unity between concept and subpart is too strong to be broken. In other words, search is not the only process involved. Material may be inapplicable even if available.

The general sequence of operations in all of the processes discussed may be represented, then, as: *search* for balance-appropriate material; *reality test* of such material (does it "make sense"? is it appropriate and realistic in context?); finally, *application* of the material (attending to it, "rehearsing" it) if it satisfies the reality test. This sequence of operations is very similar to the sequence posited by Newell, Shaw, and Simon (1959) in their theory of complex problem-solving, although the details of the individual operations are quite different.

Failure to redress imbalance. These considerations lead to a question that has not yet been raised in this chapter: What dynamic consequences will follow from the situation in which an unbalanced cognition or structure of cognitions cannot be restored to balance? In Chapter 2 Rosenberg has suggested two likely outcomes: delayed rejection of the communications on the basis of which the imbalance (or in the terms of that chapter, the "affective-cognitive inconsistency") was first aroused; [4] or if this is impossible then mechanisms of inattention and deverbalization may be employed through which the individual may avoid thinking about the imbalance. In an earlier publication (Abelson and Rosenberg, 1958) it was maintained that imbalance will be motivating, will create tension, only when it is regarded and examined, i.e. only when it is thought about.

An implication that will be merely mentioned here is that the kinds of emotional conflict whose ultimate fate is their "repression" may be understood as cognitive imbalances that cannot be resolved and are too distressing to think about. The impossibility of resolution may be due to the comparative emptiness of the appropriate "cognitive files." Thus, conflicts laid down during pre-verbal phases of personality development are probably more difficult of resolution because of the paucity of associated distinctions and differentiations by which they might be reorganized or resolved. Or such appropriate "cognitive material" though "filed" may be unavailable because of the functional stupidity and cognitive

4. Osgood and Tannenbaum (1955) represent this alternative in their concept of the "incredulity response."

rigidity that seem to occur under conditions of high anxiety such as obtain when a person is in intense conflict.

These last points, however, suggest that there is still a third possible way of adapting to certain kinds of cognitive imbalance incapable of resolution. Some unbalanced situations are quite difficult to resolve and yet quite difficult to avoid thinking about because they are central in some recurrent and manifest personal concerns of the individual. Frequently the individual will handle such unbalanced situations by alternating between thinking about them and suppressing them. "Chronic" imbalances of this sort are undoubtedly quite common (e.g. "I like to smoke but it may injure my health," or "My son has fallen in with a bad crowd of boys," or "My otherwise excellent academic job doesn't pay enough money"). The present theoretical position in no way precludes the analysis of such long-term situations.

Alternative research approaches. At least three research strategies are available by which a model such as ours may be put to further test. One of these involves the use of subjects' "real" attitudinal-cognitions about real-world issues. When such issues are chosen for study, much of the material in the subject's cognitive "files" remains unknown to the experimenter, unless special attempts are made to elicit it. Abelson and Rosenberg's "open-middled sentences" technique (1958) is one such attempt; Zajonc's (1955) listing and grouping of associations is another; [5] Smith, Bruner, and White's intensive interviews (1956) may be regarded as a more extensive, albeit less formal, method of achieving the same end. If the present model is to be applied to the investigation of "real" attitudinal cognitions new techniques will have to be devised or adapted from existing operations.

5. The Zajonc technique may also be used to modify cognitive processes. For example, Brock and Sears (1960) have conducted a preliminary investigation, using the materials of the present studies, on the effect of prior cognitive elaboration upon acceptance of countercommunications.

There are a number of problems here, not the least of which is that the subject himself may not be able to report overtly all of his associated cognitive material.

The role-playing operation used in our present experiments represents a second, and possibly new, strategy in the study of attitudinal cognitions. It was motivated by the desire to avoid the complications of idiosyncratic cognitive histories which cannot be completely compared. Thus we built into the situation as much of the relevant history as we could. It is quite likely that subjects do nevertheless attach some idiosyncratic meanings to this contrived material. However we have found in our experiments that the role-play device considerably limits extraneous variability of response. We have found too that our subjects report that they feel troubled and perplexed by situations we have classified as unbalanced, and that they claim their thoughts, while playing the role, to be representative of what they do in real life.

There is yet a third style of experimentation in this area. Instead of relying on verbal materials, one may produce cognitive imbalances by situational manipulations. Direct experience with objects or situations provides the controlled history. The experiments based on Festinger's dissonance theory (1957) are generally of this type.

All three approaches are relevant and potentially useful. It is not our intent to test the balance model only with role-playing experiments. Ultimately all three experimental styles will be used in a unified attempt to develop the theory further.

One other possibility for future work would involve developing the details of cognitive microprocesses via computer simulation. High-speed electronic computers have recently become easier to program for complex searching and processing operations (Newell, Shaw, and Simon, 1959) such as those required by the present model. Were a computer instructed to obey the mechanics of the model, we could pose unbalanced situations for the computer and observe the resolution attempts. By successive refinements of the model, the computer could in principle be made to produce responses more and more similar to those of human subjects. The advantage of such a procedure is that the abstract language required to program the machine is very similar to the kind of abstract language needed to specify microprocess theory. Such a theory is preponderantly "qualitative" rather than quantitative. Furthermore, computer simulation would very quickly expose logical inconsistencies, sins of omission, and other deficiencies in the theory by yielding implausible or nonsense "responses" in trial runs. (These considerations are discussed in detail by Reitman, 1959.) While good computer simulation is still a long way off, it offers considerable promise.

CHAPTER 5

A Dissonance Analysis of Attitude-Discrepant Behavior

JACK W. BREHM

SOMETIMES AN INDIVIDUAL engages in behavior inconsistent with his beliefs or feelings. A politician, for example, may publicly criticize socialism though he privately favors it. Or a racial segregationist may abide by integration laws. Though such discrepancies between beliefs or feelings and behavior have not been counted, they are probably frequent. It is also probable that the occurrence of such discrepancies may create in the individual some feeling of discomfort—i.e. a psychological tension of some kind. That such tensions do occur in the presence of certain types of discrepancies is recognized in our language by such words as, for example, "guilt," which names an emotional state arising from a discrepancy between one's moral or ethical values and one's behavior. Our interest here, however, is not in listing the names of such emotional states but rather in stating as generally as possible the conditions under which discrepancies between cognitions or affects and behavior will produce certain specified changes in these or other cognitions, affects, and behaviors. As a point of departure for conceptualization and explanation of relevant research, we will use Festinger's theory of cognitive dissonance (1957). (Another theoretical approach to these problems along the lines of conflict theory is being developed by a member of the Yale communications research group, Irving L. Janis.)

While the conceptual definitions of "cognition," "affect," and "behavior" are consistent with those in other parts of this volume, a distinction between cognitive and affective aspects of attitude will not always be consistently made. Few of the studies cited in the following pages allow for clear assignment of these terms to either independent or dependent variables. Thus our discussion will usually be in terms of "attitudes" even though close inspection of the research operations in question might reveal an emphasis on affect or cognition. This conceptual treatment of research data will, in most cases, be consistent with the conceptualizations utilized by the investigators.

A definition of discrepant behavior

Ordinarily an attitude—i.e. certain cognitions and/or affects about a given "object"—also implies a certain kind of behavior in regard to that object. *Discrepant behavior,* then, is either the absence of or the opposite of the implied behavior. To put it another way, a behavior X is discrepant from any attitude that implies *Not X*. The application of this definition at an operational level will become clear from the research cited in the following pages. It will be noted that this definition of discrepant behavior is similar to, and may be considered a special case of, Festinger's definition of a dissonant relationship (1957).

BACKGROUND

Suppose a town mayor privately believed that taxes should be raised though his party took the official stand that taxes should be lowered. Suppose further that his party would not support him for re-election unless he spoke out in favor of lower taxes, and party support was necessary to be assured of election. Thus to keep on good terms with his party in general and to keep his job of mayor in particular, the individual would have to argue against his private attitude on the issue of taxation. Clearly his verbal behavior would be discrepant from his private attitude. Assuming that our mayor did in fact make statements in direct disagreement with his private attitude, what might we expect in regard to his private attitude on this issue? Will it have changed, and if so, will it have moved toward consistency with his public utterances or will it have become even stronger in its original position? Furthermore, if his attitude does change in connection with his overt persuasion, what factors will increase or decrease the amount of such change? Will strong overt persuasion result in more change than weak? With such questions in mind, let us now see how dissonance theory conceptualizes the general problem, and what theoretical expectations it offers.

Dissonance theory [1] is readily applicable to the problem since, as mentioned earlier, our definition of discrepant behavior is a special case of the definition of a dissonant relationship. According to the theory, an individual who engages in discrepant behavior will experience dissonance, i.e. a psychological tension capable of motivating, among other things, attitude change. But to understand its effects, we must first examine the determinants of its strength or magnitude.

The magnitude of dissonance experienced by an individual engaging in discrepant behavior will be a function of the

1. The theoretical formulation used in this chapter is a simplification of Festinger's statement (1957), designed for ease of discussion of this particular problem area in a way consistent with the terminology in this volume. The reader is warned that there is a considerable difference between the original formulation and the present simplification: the original has more implications than the simplified version; and the simplified version might conceivably have implications unintended by the original.

strength of forces against engaging in the behavior compared to the strength of forces for engaging in it.[2] The relationship is described by the following pseudo-equation:

$$\frac{\text{Dissonance from}}{\text{discrepant behavior}} = \frac{\text{Force against engaging in behavior}}{\text{Force for engaging in behavior}}$$

where it is understood that each term is an index of strength or magnitude. The force against engaging in the behavior is a composite of (1) negative attitudes toward the behavior or its object, (2) the amount or strength of behavior involving negative attitudes, (3) positive attitudes toward alternative behaviors whose execution is prevented by the behavior in question and (4) situational restraints against engaging in the behavior, such as consequent punishment. The force in favor of engaging in the behavior is a composite of (1) positive attitudes toward the behavior or its object, (2) the amount or strength of behavior involving positive attitudes, (3) situational inducements, such as rewards, and (4) situational coercions, such as threats of punishment for noncompliance. It should be noted that the force against the behavior must always be smaller than the force in favor of it for otherwise the behavior would not occur.

It is clear from this formulation that the magnitude of dissonance will be a direct function of any of the forces against engaging in the discrepant behavior, and an inverse function of any of the forces in favor of engaging in the discrepant behavior. Thus, with other things held constant, the magnitude of dissonance will increase as the strength of the initial attitude increases, as the strength of the induced behavior increases, or as situational restraints against the behavior increase. The magnitude of dissonance will decrease as posi-

2. The magnitude of dissonance is also a function of the general or average importance (strength) of forces relevant to the behavior. We will not, however, be concerned with this variable as either a determinant or as a reducer of the magnitude of dissonance.

tive attitudes toward the discrepant behavior increase, as proffered rewards for engaging in the behavior increase, or as threatened punishments for not engaging in the behavior increase.

The theory asserts that when an individual experiences dissonance he will try to reduce or eliminate it. In general, reduction may be accomplished by change in the same variables that determine the initial magnitude of dissonance: forces against engaging in the behavior can be reduced and forces for engaging in the behavior can be increased.

Though the several possible modes of dissonance reduction can be assumed to be under equal pressure to change, some will presumably change more than others due to their having less *resistance* against change. The determinants of resistance against change appear to be complex, including, for example, the amount of social support an individual enjoys, the amount of experience the individual has had with the object in question, the individual's expertness on the issue, etc. For our purposes it will be sufficient to recognize that any variable will tend to be resistant to change to the extent that it is tied to physical or social reality (agreement with others). Thus one's own behavior, such as supporting publicly a position in disagreement with one's private view, will be relatively resistant to change since the actual behavior will have been done and misperception of it will be difficult. On the other hand, cognitive dimensions on which people disagree (e.g. opinions) or affective responses that are mainly individualistic and private in nature (e.g. object preferences) will tend to be relatively low in resistance to change. In short, some of the cognitive and affective components of attitude are likely to be the major factors involved in reduction of dissonance from discrepant behavior.

Let us return to the problem of what happens when a person expounds a view discrepant with his private attitude.

Since his initial attitude would ordinarily lead him to argue in its favor, trying to give good arguments for an opposing attitude is discrepant and will create dissonance. The resulting dissonance may be reduced in several ways, such as enhancing the negative consequences that would have occurred if he had not complied, enhancing the apparent rewards to be gained by compliance, changing his private attitude so that it more nearly agrees with what he said. It should be noted that the latter method can completely eliminate the dissonance since it erases the discrepancy between his behavior and his attitude. Whether the individual uses one of these methods or some other, the amount of his attitude change will be a function of the determinants of the magnitude of dissonance, that is, the forces for and against his making the discrepant persuasion. The greater is the magnitude of dissonance created by discrepant behavior, the greater will be the amount of attitude change.

Evidence on the general hypothesis that discrepant persuasive behavior will tend to result in attitude change toward the position it supports is available from an experiment by Kelman (1953). He had junior high school students write essays either in support of a type of comic book they favored or in support of a type they were against. Various kinds of rewards were used to induce students to write in support of the book they were against, but they will not be described here. The students' attitudes toward the comic books (as reading for younger children) were measured before and after the essays were written. Let us then compare the mean attitude change score of those subjects who wrote in support of the book they were against with the mean score of those subjects who wrote in support of the book they favored. The results showed that those supporting the initially disliked book changed more in the direction favoring it than did those who wrote in support of the liked book. One must be cautious in interpreting these results since part of the effect may be due to bias from the subjects' deciding which essay they would write; nevertheless, the results are consistent with dissonance theory. When an individual engages in persuasion discrepant with his private attitude, he will experience dissonance, and he will tend to reduce the dissonance by changing his attitude so that it more nearly agrees with (leads to) his persuasive behavior.

Further evidence on this general hypothesis comes from work by Janis and King (1954, 1956) on the attitudinal consequences of role-playing. In their first study (1954), they had college students present, as sincerely as possible, a speech from a prepared outline or listen to a speech given by another student. In all cases the position of the speech disagreed with the initial position of both the speaker and the listener. A questionnaire was used to measure attitudes both before and after the experimental inductions. The attitude change scores indicated that speech givers tended to show more opinion change toward the discrepant position upheld by the speech than did the listeners. The obtained difference is therefore consistent with the derivation of dissonance theory.

A second study (King and Janis, 1956) was designed to show the effect on attitude change of improvisation in giving the discrepant speech. In one condition, the subject was asked to read the speech silently, in a second condition, to read it aloud, and in the third, to read it silently then give it aloud (from memory) as would an impromptu speaker. Looked at from the point of view of dissonance theory, subjects in the third, improvisation group were required to put greater effort into their discrepant persuasions than were subjects in either of the other two groups. Since the inducing force was the same for all three conditions, it is clear that the magnitude of dissonance should have been a direct function of the strength of the induced discrepant behavior and, hence, should have been greater in the improvisation condition than in either of the other two conditions. The results were consistent with this analysis: net opinion change toward the position of the speech was reliably greater in the improvisation condition than in either of the other two conditions.

It should be noted, however, that this study as well as the two studies previously discussed were conducted prior to the statement of dissonance theory. Since they may have influenced to some degree the precise form of the theory, they do not test it in the same sense as does a study specifically designed to test one of the theoretical derivations, although they still stand as empirical evidence relevant to our general problem. The rest of the studies discussed in this chapter were designed to test implications of dissonance theory.

A test of one possible theoretical derivation has been conducted by Cohen, Brehm, and Fleming (1958). The hypothesis, which comes straight from our pseudo-equation, is that the amount of dissonance and consequent attitude change will be inversely related to the force inducing the discrepant persuasion. To test it, college students were asked, in a classroom setting, to write essays supporting the attitude side opposite their own on a current event issue (the desirability of introducing coeducation at Yale). In one condition they were given minimal reasons for writing the discrepant essay, while in another, they were given multiple reasons—e.g. it would help the experimenter, the school authorities, and social scientists. If it is assumed that each reason adds to the force to engage in the counter-attitudinal persuasion, then the inducing force is greater in the latter, high-justification condition than in the former, low-justification condition. The magnitude of dissonance and consequent positive atti-

tude change toward the discrepant position should therefore be greater in the condition of low, rather than high,
justification.

After elimination of the extreme scorers on the attitude
scale (for whom it is difficult to show change), the change
scores show that subjects who received low justification
changed reliably more than did those receiving high justification. These data support the proposition that, with strength
of initial attitude and required discrepant persuasion held
constant, the greater the force inducing discrepant persuasion, the less the magnitude of dissonance and consequent
attitude change in the direction of the discrepant position.

Additional evidence for the same hypothesis, but with a
different type of inducing force, comes from an experiment
by Festinger and Carlsmith (1959). Their study involved the
following steps: (1) the subject (a college student) performed
a boring and tedious task for about one hour; (2) it was then
"explained" to him that the experiment was to see how a
person's performance on these tasks was affected by his initial
set, the other condition being one in which the subject is
first told by a fake subject that he has just found the experiment to be very interesting and a lot of fun; (3) the subject
was then asked if he would perform the task of telling the
"incoming subject" that the experiment was very interesting,
since the person who usually did this could not be there;
(4) after the subject told the "incoming subject" (who in
reality was a paid participant) that the experiment was interesting and fun, he was interviewed by "a representative of the
psychology department," ostensibly to evaluate this and other
studies being done in the department. The interview was
designed to estimate how enjoyable the subject felt the performance experiment was. In one condition, subjects were
offered $1 for telling the "incoming subject" the experiment
was interesting, while in a second condition they were offered

$20 for performing the same task. In a third, control, condition, subjects were interviewed immediately after the experiment was "explained."

In terms of the theory as stated earlier, the individual who tells the incoming subject that the experiment was interesting and enjoyable is engaging in behavior discrepant from his private attitude. Since the negative attitude and required discrepant persuasion are identical in the two experimental conditions, the forces not to engage in the discrepant persuasion are equal. On the other hand, the force to perform the discrepant persuasion is a $1 reward in one condition, a $20 reward in the other. If $20 constitutes a greater inducing force than $1, the magnitude of dissonance and consequent positive attitude change toward the performance task should be less in the $20 condition than in the $1 condition.

The results for the control condition confirmed that the subjects thought the performance task somewhat unenjoyable. The measured attitude of subjects in the $20 condition was not significantly different from that for the controls. And, as expected, the measured attitude of subjects in the $1 condition was reliably more positive than that for subjects in either the $20 or control conditions. Thus with the strength of initial attitude and required discrepant persuasion held constant, the greater the inducing force that obtains the discrepant persuasion, the less the tendency to show attitude change toward the discrepant position.

In summary, the evidence on the effects of discrepant persuasion supports the general hypothesis that the persuader's attitude will change toward the position of the discrepant position, and the specific hypotheses that the amount of attitude change is (1) directly proportional to the strength of the discrepant persuasive behavior, and (2) inversely proportional to the strength of the force inducing the discrepant persuasion.

While the evidence supports dissonance theory, it leaves unanswered a series of questions pertaining to the conditions necessary for the obtained effects. In particular, it must be established whether or not *persuasive* behavior must be involved to produce the attitudinal change, whether or not a *decision* to engage in discrepant behavior (or persuasion) is sufficient, and more generally, just what factors are necessary to produce attitude change when discrepant behavior occurs.

RESEARCH EVIDENCE

The evidence so far discussed has centered on the effects of making persuasive statements that oppose one's private attitude. According to dissonance theory, however, the attitudinal effects should be about the same whether or not the discrepant behavior involves the making of persuasive statements. At the same time, as long as the evidence is confined to the effects of discrepant persuasion, it may alternatively be understood in terms of reinforcement theory as change in habit strengths due to rewards following the discrepant verbal responses. What is needed, then, is evidence concerning the attitudinal effects of *nonpersuasive* discrepant behavior, since it would not only broaden general knowledge concerning the effects of discrepant behavior, but would also bear on the issue of how to interpret or explain the various phenomena. By "nonpersuasive" is meant either verbal or nonverbal behavior that does not *require* the individual to repeat facts or arguments directly leading to the attitude change in question. It should be noted that the definition does not preclude the possibility that the individual will make implicit "persuasive" responses.

In order to examine the effects of nonpersuasive discrepant behavior, a study was designed and conducted by Brehm (1960). The plan was to induce teen-age children to eat, or commit themselves to eating, varying amounts of a disliked vegetable, to give them information about the vegetable's food value that would support or fail to support eating it, and then to measure their change in liking for the vegetable. It was assumed that commitment to eat a disliked vegetable would create dissonance, and that this could and would be reduced by increased liking for the vegetable. It was also assumed that there is nothing in the mere commitment to eat that requires persuasive statements in regard to liking.

The study to be described, aside from providing evidence on the effects of nonpersuasive discrepant behavior, has particular relevance for the view of attitude taken in this volume. It was designed to reveal affective change as a consequence of the interaction between commitment to discrepant behavior and cognitive support for the behavior. Thus it permits inspection of the interplay of all three attitudinal components under the specified conditions.

A preliminary questionnaire administered in junior high school English classes provided information about which of 34 different vegetables each student disliked. About three weeks later each student was individually sent to the homemaking room of the school, where he was informed by the experimenter that he was to take part in some "consumer research." He was asked to fill out a questionnaire about a vegetable, purportedly picked at random but actually picked as one extremely disliked by the subject. One of the questions asked the subject to indicate, on a multiple response scale, how much he liked the vegetable. A second question asked him to estimate the vitamin content using a scale with identifying labels running from "extremely below average" to "extremely above average."

When the questionnaire was finished, the experimenter told the subject that his answers were valuable but that sometimes a person gave different answers if he actually ate some of the vegetable first. The experimenter further explained that the subject did not have to eat any and could return to class if he wished, but to encourage people to eat some and answer further questions, he was offering a prize to those who did. The prize was a certificate for two phonograph records of the subject's choice, or two tickets to movies of his choice. At this point the experimenter introduced the variation in amount of behavior to which the subject committed himself. Commitment to little eating ("low-eat" condition) was accomplished by making the reward contingent on eating a single portion of the vegetable. Commitment to relatively more eating ("high-eat" condition) was accomplished by making the reward contingent on eating a portion and then returning "three or four times" to eat more of the vegetable. Almost all subjects agreed to eat and, of those refusing, there were no more in the high-eat condition than in the low. The subject was then given a small dish of the vegetable, heated if appropriate, and allowed a few minutes in which to eat it.

To vary the amount of cognitive support for engaging in the discrepant behavior, each subject was given, when finished eating, a "research report that he might be interested in reading." The report said that his vegetable was either the best or the worst for supplying the necessary vitamins in a person's diet. Finally, the subject was asked to fill out the questionnaire again, with the explanation that "some people change one way, some another, and some don't change at all."

In addition to the above procedure, a control experiment was conducted with a similar population at another school. It consisted of a preliminary questionnaire to ascertain disliked vegetables, and the administration of a booklet, one week later in the classroom, made up of the experimental questionnaire and, in a sealed section, a "research report" and another copy of the experimental questionnaire. After completion of the first questionnaire, subjects were instructed to imagine what it would be like to eat some of the vegetable, to read the research report, and then to fill out the second questionnaire. It was again explained that "some change one way, some another, and some don't change at all."

In summary, some subjects were asked to imagine what it would be like to eat the vegetable, some were asked to eat a small portion of it to obtain a reward, and some were asked to eat a small portion immediately and again later three or four times to obtain a reward. Within each of these treatments, some subjects read "supporting" research reports while others read "nonsupporting" reports. Questionnaire responses provide change scores for estimates of vitamin content (acceptance of the research report) and liking for the vegetable.

The control subjects provide an estimate of reactions to the research reports where there is no commitment to eat. Their estimates of vitamin content should increase with the support communication and decrease with the nonsupport communication. The mean estimate changes in Table 20 clearly confirm this expectation.

TABLE 20. *Mean changes in estimated vitamin content (N in parentheses)*

| | COMMUNICATION | |
Commitment	Nonsupport	Support
Control	−3.02 (11)	0.92 (10)
Low-eat	−2.35 (8)	0.77 (7)
High-eat	−0.34 (7)	1.66 (10)

It is conceivable that the research reports also might affect an individual's liking for the vegetable: support could increase liking, nonsupport decrease it. The mean changes in liking show that there is such a direct effect, the difference between the support (.46) and nonsupport (—.43) means in the control condition being significant at the 5% level by a two-tailed t-test.

Before inspecting the main results, let us consider what might be expected theoretically. Dislike of eating the vegetable is a force against committing oneself: the more eating is required, the greater the force against commitment and the greater the dissonance subsequent to commitment. Thus a research report given after commitment which supports commitment will tend to be highly accepted since it helps to reduce dissonance, while a nonsupporting report will tend to be rejected since it tends to increase dissonance. Any attempt to disbelieve the nonsupporting communication is likely to be only partly successful, however, since the content is clear and the source highly credible. The magnitude of dissonance will therefore be greater for persons receiving the nonsupporting communication than for persons receiving the supporting communication. Hence, *the pressure to reduce dissonance, and the consequent increase in liking for the vegetable, should tend to be greater from the nonsupporting than from the supporting communication.* This tendency expected from attempts to reduce dissonance is in the opposite direction to the effect of the communications observed in the control condition. The prediction in regard to increased liking, then, is that the direct effect will tend to be reduced or even reversed in the high-eat (high dissonance) condition. The effect of the low-eat condition should, of course, fall between those of the control and high-eat conditions.

The mean changes in estimated vitamin content, presented in Table 20, show that subjects in the low-eat condition reacted in a manner similar to that of the controls. On the other hand, subjects in the high-eat condition show less lowering of their vitamin estimate from the nonsupport com-

munication and greater raising of it from the support communication than do either control or low-eat subjects. If
averaged across communications, this effect is significantly
different from that in the low-eat condition at the 5% level,
and from the control condition at the 1% level. These results
tend to confirm the prediction that commitment to a relatively great amount of discrepant behavior will increase resistance to belief of a nonsupporting communication and
increase acceptance of a supporting communication.

The theoretical expectation in regard to change in liking
also receives support, as may be seen in Table 21. While the

TABLE 21. *Mean liking changes for each condition* *

| | COMMUNICATION | |
Commitment	*Nonsupport*	*Support*
Control	−.43	.46
Low-eat	.11	1.97
High-eat	1.33	.48

* p-values for various comparisons:
  Control (nonsupport-support) = .05
  Low-eat (nonsupport-support) = .06
  High-eat (nonsupport-support) = .09
  Nonsupport (high eat-control) = .02
  Nonsupport (high eat-low eat) = not sig.
  Support (low eat-control) < .01
  Support (low eat-high eat) < .01
  Low-eat (nonsupport-support)—high-eat (nonsupport-support) = .02
  Control (nonsupport-support)—high-eat (nonsupport-support) = .03

difference between support and nonsupport treatments in
the low-eat condition is similar to that in the control, the
difference in the high-eat condition is reversed. And though
the latter difference is significant at only the 9% level, it is
significantly different from the effect of the low-eat condition at the 2% level, and from the effect of the control condition at the 3% level. It is apparent, then, that the direct
effect of a communication on liking for a food tends to be

lessened in proportion to the amount of eating to which the individual is committed. Stated more generally, *the effect of cognitive support on negative affect toward the object of behavior will tend to be reversed in direct proportion to the amount of behavior to which the individual is committed.*

It will have been noted that in one respect the data of Table 21 do not at all confirm our theoretical expectations since they show no greater increase in liking among high-eat subjects in general than among low-eat subjects in general. For if dissonance affects change in liking above and beyond the direct effect of the communications on liking, then the amount of increased liking in each of the high-eat conditions should be greater than its comparison in the low-eat condition. While the reason for this failure of support is not clear, two possibilities may be suggested.

The first is that, although the interaction among the four experimental conditions reflects the operation of dissonance as hypothesized, there has been an additional factor introduced between the high-and low-eat conditions that differentially affects the ease of change in liking. For example, subjects in the high-eat condition are contemplating further eating of the food, which may reduce their ability to re-evaluate it, whereas subjects in the low-eat condition have eaten all that is required and may feel less tied to reality in making their evaluations. In any case, if there is a complicating factor of this type in the commitment manipulation, then our general conclusions about the effect of behavioral commitment and cognitive support on affect would remain unchanged.

The second suggested reason for the lack of over-all difference between the high- and low-eat conditions is that the direct effect of the communications on liking is itself due to dissonance arising from the discrepancy between the behavioral commitment and the information received. In the low-eat condition, where the amount of committed eating is relatively slight, the information in support of eating is discrepant and produces dissonance which in turn is reduced by increased liking. The nonsupporting information is, of course, perfectly consistent with the small amount of behavior committed in the low-eat condition and thus produces no dissonance or change in liking; while in the control condition, where there is no behavioral commitment at all, the change in liking is completely consistent with the information, increasing with support and decreasing with nonsupport.

The crucial implication of the notion that the direct effect of the communications results from dissonance is that, in the support treatment, the commitment to a large amount of eating will tend to reduce the dissonance just as the supporting communication tends to reduce the dissonance aroused by the commitment to a large amount of eating. Thus the conditions which separately produce high dissonance, high-eat and support, together reduce each other's dissonance and thus produce very little increase in liking. In this case, then, the commitment and information variables are assumed to interact in arousing dissonance and consequent increase in liking, while in the first explanation the simple effect of the information on liking was assumed to be *additive* with the dissonance aroused by the conjunction of the commitment and information variables.

Regardless of these alternative interpretations, the data show that *nonpersuasive* discrepant behavior has attitudinal consequences similar to those of persuasive. They thus give additional support to dissonance theory and at the same time make more difficult any explanation that depends on reinforcement of persuasive responses.

Related evidence

Further evidence on the effects of nonpersuasive discrepant behavior comes from an experiment by Mills (1958) in which he studies the effects of cheating or being honest on attitudes toward cheating. He offered grade school children prizes for good performance on simple tasks. Three experimental conditions were created; high temptation to cheat with low restraint against doing so; low temptation with low restraint; and high temptation with high restraint. Temptation was manipulated by offering or not offering a prize either for an outstanding score or for improvement from a preliminary practice session. Restraints against cheating were manipulated by giving the subjects differential opportunity to cheat while scoring their own work. Attitudes toward cheating were measured before and after this procedure. Attitudes of a control group were measured twice without the intervening experimental procedure.

In terms of dissonance theory, a restraining force against the behavior engaged in by an individual has the same dissonance-creating effect as does a negative attitude toward the behavior. Thus an individual who cheats will experience dissonance in proportion to the strength of restraint against cheating. And as with other induced behavior, the amount of dissonance created will decrease as the inducing force (temptation to cheat) is increased. Whatever dissonance is created from cheating in the presence of inducing and restraining forces can be reduced or eliminated by attitude change favoring cheating. A similar analysis applies to those persons who behave honestly. The magnitude of dissonance and consequent attitude change against cheating will be a *direct* function of the inducing force (temptation to cheat) and an *inverse* function of the restraining force (which supports being honest).

The attitude change scores indicate that cheaters tended to become more lenient toward cheating and honest subjects tended to become more critical of cheating. While the pattern of results also tends to support the predicted effects of variations in temptation and restraints, it does not provide consistently reliable evidence. It is clear, however, that subjects' attitudes toward cheating did change in a direction consistent with their behavior.

It should be noted that the attitude change in this study is not necessarily discrepancy-reducing. Honest subjects presumably had a strong attitude against cheating prior to the experiment or they would have cheated when tempted. What was discrepant for them was being honest when it might cause them to miss obtaining an attractive prize. Thus the result of a behavioral discrepancy may be the strengthening of an attitude already consistent with the behavior.

A study by Aronson and Mills (1959) furnishes further support for the general hypothesis that nonpersuasive discrepant behavior creates dissonance and consequent attitude change. In our terms their specific hypothesis was that the greater the force against engaging in a given behavior, the greater the resulting dissonance and consequent attitude change toward support of the behavior. In this case, however, the force against engaging in the behavior was itself an unpleasant behavior.

Female college students were required to take an "embarrassment" test in order to join a sex discussion group for which they had volunteered. Each subject in the low-force condition was required to read a list of objective sex-related words to the male experimenter. Each subject in the high-force condition was required to read a list of obscene sex-related words to the same experimenter. Subsequent to the test the subject audited a purported group discussion, actually tape-recorded, which was designed to be dull and uninteresting. Finally, subjects were asked to indicate how good they thought the discussion and how much they liked the group members.

Having a favorable attitude toward the discussion and the group constitutes a force on the individual to join the group: hence, dissonance created by engaging in the embarrassment test in order to get into the group can be reduced by *increased* favorable attitude toward the discussion and group members. The more embarrassing or painful the test to get in the group, the more dissonance is created and the greater should be the increased favorable attitude.

The results show that attitudes of subjects in the mild embarrassment condition were not different from those of control subjects who took no test, while attitudes of subjects in the severe embarrassment condition were more favorable than those of either the control or mild test groups. These differences tend to confirm the general notion that the greater the force against engaging in the behavior, the greater the amount of dissonance created and the greater the resultant attitude change in support of the behavior. And, in the present case, the force against engaging in the behavior was itself an unpleasant behavior, thus further broadening the class of discrepant events known to have implications for attitude change.

The support for the dissonance theory interpretation of the attitudinal consequences of induced discrepant behavior may now be summarized.

1. The induction of behavior counter to other attitudinal components (cognitive and/or affective) tends to result in cognitive and/or affective change toward consistency with or support of the behavior.

a. The inducing force may be an attitude, a reward, a verbal justification, an implicit or explicit request, etc.

b. The attitudinal component changed need not be involved in the original discrepancy. According to dissonance theory, it must be relevant to the behavior and the change should be toward increased support of the behavior.

2. The greater the magnitude of force inducing the discrepant behavior, the less the amount of consequent attitude change.

3. The greater the strength of the discrepant behavior, the greater the amount of consequent attitude change.

a. This effect will be reduced to the extent that there is additional information in support of engaging in the behavior.

4. The greater the force against engaging in a given behavior, the greater the amount of attitude change.

Limiting conditions

It seems likely that under certain conditions, discrepancies between a person's attitudinal components may not result in dissonance and consequent attempts at attitude change. This issue may be treated more generally as a discussion of the limiting conditions under which dissonance and consequent attitude change will tend to occur.

At the conceptual level it is clear that attitude change will be a function of two factors: (1) motivation to change the attitude and (2) restraints against changing the attitude. Under the latter category would come the inability to rationalize an opinion change, lack of control over one's own behavior, insufficient power to change one's environment, conflicting discrepancy-reduction tendencies, etc. Though many of these restraining factors may affect attitude change, the following discussion will be limited to the area for which research is available, namely, the *motivation* to change.

The effect of choice. Festinger's statement of dissonance theory (1957), which has served as an adequate explanation for most of the evidence so far discussed, is ambiguous about the effect of choice on the tendency to reduce discrepancies. It clearly states that where a choice is made between mutually exclusive alternatives of approximately equal attraction, dissonance and consequent re-evaluation of alternatives will take place. This assertion has been supported by experimental evidence (Brehm, 1956; Brehm and Cohen, 1959a). It would also suggest, however, that with discrepant persuasive behavior, the *decision* to take the discrepant stand is sufficient to create the dissonance and consequent attitude change. An additional question may then be raised about whether discrepant persuasion affects the amount of attitude change: such verbalization could conceivably facilitate change by helping the individual to convince himself of the validity of the dissonance-reducing position, or it could conceivably inhibit change by making the individual aware of, and defensive about, his inconsistency.

The effect of persuasive verbalization on dissonance-reducing attitude change has been studied by Rabbie, Brehm, and Cohen (1959). College students were individually asked to write an essay against intercollegiate athletics. Half of them were given high, half low, justification for writing the counter-attitudinal persuasion. To determine the effect of actually making the discrepant persuasion, half of each justification group was given the attitude measure *before* writing the essay, and the other half was given it *afterward*. A post-experimental questionnaire check on the justification manipulation indicated it was successful.

Comparison of the mean attitude scores revealed that the low-justification group attitude was reliably more positive than that of the high-justification group only where the attitude was measured *before* the essay was written. The mean difference in attitude scores between high- and low-justification groups for those receiving the attitude measure *after* writing was almost as large. It did not approach statistical significance, however, since the variability in response of these subjects was much greater than for those who wrote the essay afterward. Therefore, the results of this study failed to show that discrepant persuasion produces attitude change above and beyond the effects of dissonance. Nevertheless, the act of verbalizing the discrepant stand did produce greater variability of response, indicating that it sometimes increases, sometimes decreases, the effect.

Though this study failed to show any main effect of discrepant persuasion, it did demonstrate that a *decision* to engage in discrepant persuasion is sufficient to produce dissonance and consequent attitude change. But though the decision is sufficient, we still do not know whether it is *necessary* to the creation of dissonance and its consequences. Suppose, for example, that an individual is confronted with an event having negative consequences for him, and its occurrence is outside of his control. There would be a discrepancy between his knowledge of the impending event and his negative evaluation of it. The question is whether this discrepancy would create dissonance since the individual has no choice about whether it will happen to him. If dissonance were created, it would presumably motivate the individual to re-evaluate the impending event so as to reduce the discrepancy—i.e. minimize his negative attitude toward the event.

A study designed to answer one aspect of this question was conducted by Brehm (1959). Included as part of the food preference study reported earlier, it utilized the same general procedure and guise of consumer research. Junior high school students were asked to fill out a questionnaire about a disliked vegetable, induced to eat a small portion of it, then asked to fill out the same questionnaire again. In the control condition, each subject was asked to eat a single small portion of the vegetable in order to obtain the standard reward of phonograph records or movie tickets. The experimental condition was designed to create a *fait accompli*—i.e. an event over which the individual had no control—which, if known about beforehand, might have made the subject refuse to take part in the experiment. This was done by telling the subject when he was nearly finished eating that among the reports to be issued was a letter informing his parents which vegetable he ate. The direct implication was that he would have to eat more at home. Pre-experimental questionnaire data, to be explained below, help to confirm this interpretation.

Analysis of the liking change scores showed that there was a greater increase in liking for the vegetable in the *fait accompli* than in the control condition. The difference was significant at the 1% level. Thus a disliked event outside the individual's control can result in positive affect change toward that event, at least under the conditions of this experiment.

It might be argued that a letter home is an endorsement of the vegetable by the consumer organization, and directly affects liking. Analysis in terms of pre-questionnaire data, however, showed that the difference in liking change occurred mainly for subjects who reported they ate the vegetable at home less frequently than it was served. In other words, the *fait accompli* is effective in producing attitude change only where it has unpleasant implications. It is therefore clear that the difference in affect change is not produced by differential endorsement.

These data show that a discrepant event outside the individual's control can create dissonance and result in a tendency for attitude change. This effect may or may not be found in other general conditions. In particular, these results occurred for the induction of behavior toward which there was negative affect, where the inducement involved positive affect (a reward), and *where there was a choice just prior to the negative event.* Thus while the event does not have to be known or expected at the time of choice, prior choice may still be necessary to the creation of dissonance and the resultant tendency to change one or more attitudes.

In order to specify further the necessary conditions, a study was designed and conducted by Brehm and Cohen (1959b). It incorporated two manipulated variables and a specified general condition. The first of the manipulated variables, intended to produce variations in amount of choice felt by subjects about whether to take part in an unpleasant study, was a coercive force. This was in contrast to the use of reward in previous studies. The second variable, intended to extend knowledge of the kind of discrepant social stimuli that could lead to attitude change, was information about how others in the same experiment were to be treated. This information was designed to create a feeling in the subject of high or low deprivation compared to other subjects (i.e. "relative deprivation" as defined by Merton and Kitt, 1950). To examine further the limits of necessary conditions, the relative deprivation treatment was given to subjects as a "chance" effect. As such, it is another type of event over which the individual has no control. Furthermore, it was not like simple gambling behavior in that the subject did not know, until after he had committed himself, that his fate in this regard depended on chance. Any effect on attitude change of the relative deprivation variable would tend to confirm that *an unforeseen chance event* can affect the magnitude of dissonance.

In brief, the experiment consisted of an announcement in introductory psychology classes that all students would have to participate in a boring and tedious project, copying random numbers for three hours. An attempt was made to manipulate the coercive force to comply by saying nothing about being excused in some classes, while in others saying that a person who felt he must be excused could make an appointment with the Director of Undergraduate Studies. After subjects had signed schedule sheets committing themselves to participation, they were asked to fill out "evaluation questionnaires." The instructions for these questionnaires included the manipulation of relative deprivation. Subjects were informed by them that while most subjects would be paid for participation, a few would not, just to see what effect that might have on the copying behavior. Some instruction sheets said that subjects were being paid $1 (low relative deprivation) and other sheets said $10 (high relative deprivation). In all cases, the instruction sheet said that the subject was one of those who, *picked at random,* would not receive anything. The questionnaire was designed to check the success of the experimental manipulations and measure the subjects' satisfaction with their assignment.

The check on the coercion manipulation indicated that there was little difference between conditions. It also indicated that there were large differences between subjects within conditions. Thus the attempt to manipulate the amount of coercive force failed, but triggered large individual differences in the perceived ease with which subjects felt they could avoid participation. Analysis of the results was therefore carried out by splitting subjects within each condition at the median according to how difficult they thought it would be to get excused. Thus the analysis is in terms of *perceived* choice rather than manipulated coercive force. Responses on the after-questionnaire indicated the relative deprivation manipulation was completely successful.

According to the notion of relative deprivation (Merton and Kitt, 1950), the better off one's peers are relative to oneself, the less satisfied one will be with one's own assignment. But according to the present view, this direct effect of relative deprivation on satisfaction may occur only when the individual feels he has no choice concerning his assignment. When, on the other hand, a person does feel he has some choice or control in regard to his assignment, he should experience dissonance and exhibit the tendency to change one or more attitudes so that they more strongly support his behaviorial commitment. Thus, *choice* to engage in an unpleasant behavior will tend to be accompanied by relatively high satisfaction. In summary, if the degree of perceived choice determines the direction of attitudinal reaction to relative deprivation, then there should be an interaction among satisfaction scores that is a function of degree of perceived choice and amount of relative deprivation.

The results clearly confirm this expectation. For subjects who perceived little or no choice in regard to the unpleasant assignment, the greater the amount of relative deprivation, the lower their satisfaction with the assignment. On the other hand, for subjects who perceived relatively high choice, the greater the relative deprivation, the higher their satisfaction.

These data support the general hypothesis that the more choice a person feels in response to pressures to engage in an unpleasant behavior, the greater will be the magnitude of dissonance he experiences and, consequently, the more he will tend to reduce discrepancies between his engaging in that behavior and his attitude toward it. They suggest that subjective feelings of choice are central to the creation of dissonance and the consequent tendency to change attitudes. However, since subjective choice was not a function of the coercion manipulation, the data do not necessarily suggest that the magnitude of dissonance or the tendency to reduce discrepancies is a function of coercive force.

Since the relative deprivation was by "chance," the results of this experiment further confirm the generalization that an unforeseen event at the choice point can, even when outside the individual's control, create dissonance and affect attitudes.

Further evidence on the effect of choice comes from an experiment by Cohen, Terry, and Jones (1959). Each subject was individually contacted at his dormitory room and asked to take part in a survey. His attitude on a current campus topic of interest was then measured. After that he was read some information supporting the side opposite to that of his own attitude. To manipulate the amount of choice the subject felt concerning whether or not to listen, the experimenter said that he was going to read it (low choice) or he said that it was completely up to the subject whether or not he should read it (high choice). Only three subjects out of the 35 in the high-choice condition refused to listen (and were eliminated from the analysis of data). After the countercommunication had been heard, subjects were asked to fill out another questionnaire, which again measured their attitude on the issue and also obtained evidence on the success of the manipulation. The after-questionnaire check on the choice manipulation indicated it was highly successful. The data were analyzed in terms of extremity of the subjects' initial positions on the issue in order to gain information about the variable of discrepancy size. It was assumed that greater initial extremity represented greater discrepancy from the countercommunication.

Of subjects given a low amount of choice about exposure to the counter-information, those most discrepant tended to show less change toward the position of the communication than did those less discrepant. This trend is likely caused by increasing resistance against change as extremity of initial position increases. However, for subjects given high choice, the greater the discrepancy, the greater the amount of change toward the counter position. The latter difference was significantly different from the former at the 2% level.

This obtained interaction between discrepancy (initial position) and degree of choice is consistent with the theory. The greater the strength of the initial attitude, with the strength of the discrepant behavior held constant, the greater the magnitude of dissonance and consequent attitude change toward consistency with the discrepant behavior. However, the present results have shown that *this relationship is a direct function of the amount of choice* involved in engaging in the discrepant behavior.

In summary, these experiments have provided evidence that choice is a central variable in determining the magnitude of dissonance and the consequent tendency to reduce discrepancies between attitudes and behavioral commitments. The variable of choice (either manipulated or perceived) affects reactions to events ranging from those presumably taken into account at the choice point to those which are not even suspected and which occur by chance subsequent to the choice point. It may well be that wherever there is choice or a feeling of choice in relation to behavior discrepant with attitudes or situational events, dissonance will be created and consequent attitude change will tend to occur.

IMPLICATIONS

While the various studies cited in this discussion have done much to establish just what a discrepancy is and what some of its consequences may be, they have provided only a little information about the limiting conditions for these effects. At present the most adequate theory is Festinger's statement of cognitive dissonance (1957). However, some of the present research and many of the emergent problems arise from ambiguities in that theory. In the remainder of the chapter some of the major issues in question are discussed.

The role of choice. The evidence indicates that attitude change tends to occur if (1) there is a choice between attractive alternatives or (2) there is the opportunity for an implicit or explicit choice where conflicting positive and negative forces are operating on the individual or (3) there has been a choice or a feeling of choice just prior to the introduction of negative affect or cognitions. More generally, the prediction of attitude change from discrepant behavior requires an understanding of the conditions under which the individual feels he has, or at least has had, the option to avoid the discrepancy.

The discrepancy-producing force. It is clear that, at least in some cases, the amount of choice the individual has should be a function of the magnitude of the force inducing him to behavioral commitment. To induce an unpleasant behavior, for example, a reward may be offered. If the reward is too small, the individual will decline to take part. It would seem that increasing the size of the reward up to the amount necessary to induce compliance would increase subjective feelings of choice. Increasing the reward above that necessary to induce compliance would tend to decrease choice; the individual would increasingly be "forced" to comply in order to get the reward. Thus there is presumably a close relationship between the size of the inducing reward and the amount of subjective choice, though this assumption still needs direct verification.

A similar analysis might apply to coercive forces, except that some doubt was suggested by the failure of the coercive manipulation in the experiment by Brehm and Cohen (1959b). The large individual differences in perceived choice in that study point to a more complicated process. It seems likely that factors other than those intended entered into the determination of subjective choice. It may be, for example, that the apparent legitimacy or believability of the attempted coercion varied greatly among the subjects. It may also be that coercion produces a side effect of resistance in some subjects which paradoxically increases the feeling of choice. Whatever the explanation, it seems likely that the relationship between coercive forces and subjective choice may not be so simple as that assumed between rewarding forces and subjective choice.

More generally, it may be that the relationship between the discrepancy-producing force and subjective choice can vary from positive to negative, depending on the conditions under which the force is applied. To the extent, for example, that either an offered reward or a threatened punishment is seen as illegitimate, an increase in that force may only create a greater feeling of subjective choice. If it is true that attitude change tendencies are a function of subjective choice, then increased force might, under such conditions, result in increased rather than decreased attitude change.

The role of commitment. Even where there is choice, whether it be in an approach-avoidance, avoidance-avoidance, or double approach-avoidance situation, an actual decision must be made before an attitude is changed. That is, the individual must *commit* himself to a course of action (or nonaction). It seems likely that such commitment is crucial to the tendency for attitude change. Furthermore, commitment is not necessarily identical with subjective choice, though conceptual discrimination may be difficult at points. For example, commitment to a set of values, to a way of behaving, to certain attitudes, could be acquired by a learning process (such as during the socialization period of a child's life). While the individual may thus never *choose* certain values, attitudes, etc. for himself, he may nevertheless feel quite committed to them. And as a consequence of commitment, he may tend to change attitudes as a function of discrepancies that occur in regard to his other cognitions, affects, and behaviors. Thus we might say that choice tends to create commitment, but is not *necessary* to the creation of commitment.

If commitment should turn out to be a crucial variable in determining the consequences of behavioral discrepancies, then it would be necessary to investigate the relationships between forces producing discrepant behaviors and amount of resultant commitment. It is possible, for example, that inducement of unpleasant behavior with a reward may produce more commitment than inducement of the same behavior by a threat of punishment.

Many other problems could be mentioned though they have not been formulated in precise terms. It is not clear, for example, whether passive behavior such as listening to a radio program carries the same potentialities for attitude change tendencies as the active types of behavior utilized in the experimental studies discussed. Nor is it evident what effect repeated exposure to discrepancies may have. Furthermore, there has been little investigation of the possible methods by which discrepancies (or the motivation produced by them) may be reduced: some methods, such as cognitive restructuring, for example, could be more effective than others. And finally it should be mentioned that to date very little is known about individual differences in reaction to discrepancies between behavior and cognitions or affect.

While many problems have been raised by the theoretical and empirical investigations into the consequences of behavioral discrepancies, some have been solved at least in part. It seems fairly safe to say that when a person's behavioral component disagrees with his cognitive and affective components, the latter will tend to change toward support of the behavior. It is also apparent that the stronger the discrepant behavioral component, the stronger the tendency to bring the cognitive and affective components into line with it. And, if the theory of cognitive dissonance should continue to receive support, then we may say that, in general, the tendency to change a cognitive and/or affective component will be a direct function of the force against engaging in the behavior compared to the force for it.

CHAPTER 6

Summary and Further
Theoretical Issues

CARL I. HOVLAND AND MILTON J. ROSENBERG

DESPITE THE DIVERSITY of methods and theoretical formulations in the foregoing there is a substantial body of findings on factors affecting the extent and resolution of discrepancies between various beliefs and between belief, affect, and behavior. Some of the generalizations provided by the experiments are summarized and discussed in the pages below. At the same time a number of issues remain which only further research can resolve. Some of the major theoretical problems disclosed by our researches and those of other investigators in this area are discussed in the second portion of this chapter.

RESULTS

Effects of affect modification upon beliefs

The issue examined by Rosenberg in Chapter 2 is the interaction between feelings and beliefs. His starting point is the homeostatic postulate that the affective and cognitive components of an attitude tend toward a stable state of mutual consistency; if a person "likes" an object or state of affairs,

198

he may be expected to have cognitions relating the object to the attainment of desired ends. Similarly, if a person is persuaded that a particular object or state of affairs will further some end or value he favors, he will tend to increase his "liking" for the object. The arousal of affective-cognitive inconsistency to a degree in excess of the person's tolerance level is conceived as a basis for the production of attitude change. Previous studies investigating changes of feelings toward objects after beliefs have been altered are cited, but here the contrary sequence is studied: changes in affect are induced and corresponding changes in beliefs evaluated. Post-hypnotic suggestion is the means used to carry out this purpose.

The first experiment reported by Rosenberg used eleven subjects, selected from a group of professional and graduate students for their deep hypnotizability; an equal number of students was assigned to a control group. First, all subjects were given a questionnaire which elicited affective responses to seven social issues. The final session took place a week or two later. At this time, the experimental subject's cognitive structure for one of his two high-interest attitude objects was tested, and he was then hypnotized and given a suggestion of affect change for that attitude object. After the completion of the cognitive testing the control subjects merely rested in the same physical setting as the experimental subjects; in another part of the experiment, they were asked to role-play a change in their attitudes.

During the hypnotic session, each experimental subject was commanded to *feel* differently toward an object: e.g. "When you awake you will be very much in favor of the idea of Negroes moving into white neighborhoods. The mere idea will make you happy." Subjects were also told they would have no memory of the suggestion having been made until a signal was given. Upon awakening from hypnosis (or, in the case of the control subjects, after the period of rest), the subject once again was tested with the affect questionnaire and then given the cognitive structure test. The latter asked the subject to rate each of 31 values as to its importance for him and also as to the extent to which the particular value was either furthered or blocked by the attitude object— housing desegregation, or any one of six other social issues. An "index of cognitive structure" was obtained by determining the algebraic sum of the products obtained by multiplying the importance rating of each value term by its instrumentality rating.

The results of the experiment showed that the hypnotic subjects had affect change scores on the manipulated issues that were significantly different in the predicted direction from those of the control subjects. As for the major prediction, concerning *belief* changes, the results showed that the hypnotic subjects underwent more cognitive change, as measured by the index described above, than did the controls. Other results indicated that these changes were experienced as real by the experimental subjects. Thus the experiment confirmed the prediction that:

1. *When the affective component of an individual's attitude is altered, there occurs a corresponding and consistent reorganization of his beliefs about the object of that affect.* It is postulated that this effect occurs only when the degree of affective-cognitive inconsistency exceeds an assumed threshold level.

A second experiment employed similar manipulation and testing procedures. It examined the effects of a subject's remaining under the influence of a posthypnotic suggestion of affect change (on the issue of "foreign aid") for a full week, rather than just one or two hours. The affect questionnaire and the cognitive structure procedure were administered six times; each time the subject was required to "think out loud" as he answered the latter measure, so that any changes in the meaning of the value terms and the relationships between the attitude object and the value could be detected. The last two testing sessions were on the third and tenth day respectively after the hypnotist had removed the posthypnotic amnesia.

The results of this study show that the cognitive changes observed are not transient but that:

2. *As long as the reversed affect persists, the individual maintains the cognitive structure which has been reorganized in directions consistent with that reversed affect.*

The other question the present study investigated was whether thinking up new arguments to support the changed affect, and holding them for a week, affects the person's attitude after he has returned to normal. The question may be answered affirmatively. While on the tenth day after amnesia removal the subjects were closer to their original positions than they had been on the third day, they still had not returned to the point at which they had been before the start of the experiment. Thus:

3. *Some cognitive effects of affect reversal persist after the affect-reversing force has been withdrawn.* Rosenberg interprets the persistence of some of the altered cognitions as due to a kind of "self-persuasion" process; i.e. the new information and arguments that the subject evokes in his initial attempts at cognitive reorganization act back upon him to further stabilize the new cognitions.

In both of the above studies, the author was interested in the means by which cognitive changes were carried out, as well as in testing the major predictions. Two possible ways of reorganizing cognitions are changing the perceived relationships between the attitude object and values and changing the assessed desirability of those values. Both types are found to occur to a significant degree but evidence not detailed in the chapter suggests that the former is more fully used than the latter and this finding supports a "cognitive balance" analysis of the general phenomenon.

Resolution of inconsistent beliefs

Two quite different ways of looking at the problem of relationships between beliefs are presented by McGuire in Chapter 3 and by Rosenberg and Abelson in Chapter 4. McGuire, using as his reference point the expected logical relationships between beliefs, studies consistency in terms of logical thinking and wishful thinking. Logical thinking is the tendency for a person's beliefs to be in accord with each other in the pattern demanded by the rules of formal logic; thus, if a person accepts the major and minor premises of a syllogism, he is thinking logically to the extent that he agrees also with the conclusion. Wishful thinking, as conceptualized by McGuire, acts in opposition to logical thinking; it is the tendency for a person's beliefs to be in accord with his desires.

McGuire makes these tendencies operational in the following way. The individual's belief system is seen as being reducible to a series of propositions. Each proposition follows from several others and gives rise in its turn to still more. A measure of wishful thinking is obtained by asking the person to indicate on a five-point scale how desirable, regardless of truth or likelihood, he considers the state of affairs posited in the proposition to be. Then he is asked to estimate how probable he thinks it is that the statement is true. A high correlation between one's desire for a statement to be true and its actual evaluation as being true represents wishful thinking.

If the latter procedure is followed for all the propositions that make up a syllogism, one may make a quantitative estimate of how probable the individual should rate the conclusion, based on his estimates of how true the major and minor premises are, and then one may compare the truth value actually assigned by the person to the conclusion. The greater the difference between the obtained and the predicted value, the greater the person's deviation from truly logical thinking. McGuire hypothesizes that such deviation will be caused by wishful thinking; i.e. conclusions which are more desirable than their premises will receive greater estimates of being true than logic requires, while conclusions which are less desirable than their premises will be rated as less probable than they should be.

Using the above operations, McGuire studies the implications for attitude change of the logical relationships between beliefs. Specifically, he investigates the assumptions underlying the "Socratic method" of persuasion; namely, that merely eliciting a person's beliefs, and thereby revealing inconsistencies in them, will cause him to change those beliefs in the direction of greater consistency. A second question deals with the effects of introducing a persuasive communication: Will the influence of a message vary according to whether it increases or decreases the logical consistency of the person's beliefs?

An experiment dealing with these and other questions consisted of two sessions one week apart; during the first session, subjects' initial ratings as to the likelihood and desirability of related events were obtained; during the second session, persuasive messages arguing for the likelihood of certain of the events were communicated, and the subjects' cognitions were again measured.

The questionnaires by means of which these ratings were obtained presented 27 to 72 propositions whose likelihood was to be indicated on the probability measure mentioned previously. Among these statements were several sets of triads, each of which constituted a syllogism; the propositions making up any one syllogism were dispersed throughout the questionnaire. The desirability ratings were obtained by having the subjects evaluate all the propositions in terms of five response categories ranging from "very desirable" to "very undesirable."

McGuire's principal findings may be briefly summarized:

4. *Querying the individual's opinions on logically related issues, as in the Socratic method, results in a greater consistency of beliefs.* During the initial session of an experiment, there was considerable inconsistency in the subjects' estimates of the truth value of major and minor premises and conclusions. When they were asked to indicate their beliefs again one week later, the beliefs shifted into a pattern of greater mutual consistency. This change occurred without any persuasive communication or mention of belief consistency. (Regression was also ruled out as an explanation.)

5. *Individuals are more highly persuasible by messages arguing in a direction which increases consistency and are more resistant to those arguing in a direction that increases inconsistency.* McGuire hypothesizes that beliefs would initially be distorted by wishful thinking, so that desirable propositions would be believed to be more true than related but rather undesirable propositions. Thus a message arguing for the truth of a relatively desirable premise would, if accepted, increase the disparity between that premise and the related less desirable one. From this it would follow that acceptance of such a message would push the person in an inconsistency-increasing direction and hence would be resisted. On the other hand, a message arguing for the truth of an undesirable premise would push the person's beliefs into greater consistency, and hence would have more of a persuasive impact.

To test these predictions, subjects were presented with eight syllogisms, half of which had relatively desirable premises, while the rest had relatively undesirable premises. The subjects were then given communications arguing for the increased truth of the minor premise of each syllogism. The result was that the messages did in fact have a greater effect on the undesirable statements; the truth ratings of the latter increased by about 24 points on a 100 point scale, as opposed to an increase of about 14 points for the desirable statements, a significant difference.

6. *Changes produced through reduction of inconsistency on derivative unmentioned issues, while significant, are less than the amount to be expected from the logical model.* Since any given belief is related to other beliefs, a message which leads a person to change his mind on one issue should, to the extent he is motivated to be consistent, change his mind on logically related but not explicitly mentioned issues. It seems reasonable, however, to predict that this effect will not be as strong as a change brought about by an explicit communication.

The experiment testing these predictions took place in three sessions. In the first, subjects indicated their belief in the truth of propositions comprising 16 syllogisms. In the second session they received communications arguing for the truth of each of the 16 minor premises (the major premises and conclusions being unmentioned) and then indicated their immediate postcommunication belief in each of the 48 propositions. In the third session, subjects were again asked for their beliefs, to give an indication of the delayed impact of the messages. The results confirmed the prediction; the messages caused change on logically related unmentioned issues, but not as great as the change on explicit issues.

The other model for cognitive processes, proposed by Rosenberg and Abelson, involves the study of balance within and between cognitions about an emotionally significant issue. This model asserts that cognitive elements ("actors," "means," and "ends") may be related to each other in three ways: these relations can be positive, negative, or null. The basic units or "sentences" of cognitive structures are "bands" composed of pairs of elements, connected by a term defining their relationship. For example, ApB means that a positive relation exists between A and B and may denote any of the following more specific statements: person A likes person B; means A brings about end B; end A justifies means B, etc.

A and B are assumed to have "signs" attached to them; that is, they elicit positive or negative affect depending on whether they are liked or disliked. A band is balanced when the relationship between two elements is consistent with their signs. Cognitive structures are composed of numbers of bands each of which is connected to the rest by means of a common element shared with at least one other band. These structures may be balanced or unbalanced depending on the bands that make them up.

If a cognitive structure is unbalanced, and the person becomes aware of the inconsistency, he may attempt to redress the imbalance by changing relations and/or signs, by redefining the elements, or, if all else fails, by stopping thinking. Rosenberg and Abelson posit a hierarchy of such responses and report two experiments intended to test the model and its implications for the resolution of belief dilemmas.

In one experiment a large number of undergraduate subjects had such dilemmas implanted in them by means of a role-playing situation. They were given a pamphlet inviting them to take the role of a department store owner who placed positive value on keeping sales at a high level. The subjects in one of three groups were told they also felt positively toward two other "concepts," modern art, and the manager of the rug department, Fenwick. In the second group modern art was positive and Fenwick negative, while in the third, both concepts were given negative signs.

In addition, subjects were assigned "beliefs" about the relations between the three concepts. All were told that they believed the following: Displays of modern art in department stores reduce sales volume; Fenwick plans to have such a display in the rug department; Fenwick's management has in the past increased the volume of rug sales.

Thus, by assigning to each of the three groups cognitive structures identical in asserted relations but varying in the evaluations of the things related, three cognitive structures are set up, each unbalanced in a different locus (i.e. on a different band). In the first structure, with all concepts positively evaluated, the band involving the belief that displays of modern art reduce sales volume is the unbalanced one; in the second structure, with modern art negatively evaluated, the band involving the belief that Fenwick plans to display modern art is unbalanced; in the third, with both Fenwick and modern art negative, it is the belief that he has increased sales that is unbalanced. The simplest, or least effortful, way to restore balance would be to change the relation in the unbalanced band.

The subjects were then presented with three "countercommunications" said to have issued from three store officers. Each of these presented "information" which, if accepted, would lead to the least effortful solution for one of the three unbalanced cognitive structures, i.e. the solution involving only one change in relation rather than some plural number of relation and sign changes. (It was assumed that the three relations were originally of equal intensity. However, when this is not the case the least effortful change might be to accept a communication calling for reversal of a weakly established relation even if this in turn required an additional change in the sign of one of the concepts.) When subjects were asked to indicate how much they were pleased and persuaded by each communication and how accurate they thought it was, the results were in line with predictions from the model; thus:

7. *The preferred solution to a belief dilemma is one involving the least effortful path.*

In a second study using revised forms of the dilemmas described above, the aim was to examine more closely changes in the cognitive structures themselves, and also to find out whether subjects who accept a potentially balance-restoring communication actually go on to balance their cognitions in the expected way. This was done by means of a questionnaire given twice during the experimental session—after the assigned structure had been presented and again after the evaluation of the countercommunication had been completed. The questionnaire asked subjects to rate on an eleven-point scale ranging from extremely negative to extremely positive the three concepts, high sales volume, modern art, and Fenwick, and the relations between them.

An interesting finding was that some of the subjects were enough disturbed by the imbalance to set to work to undo it as soon as the dilemma was communicated, before the presentation of the countercommunications. But the main finding of the present experiment was that in addition to a "force" propelling the person toward the redress of unbalanced states, there is a second force propelling him in the direction of maximum hedonic gain—a sort of "pleasure principle," which may work either in concert with or in opposition to the consistency principle. Thus, it was found that when the least effortful means of attaining balance was also the most hedonic, it was more likely to be accepted and incorporated into the person's cognitive structure. In the first structure, for example, by accepting the belief that modern art is good for sales, the person ends up with the consistent and pleasant set of beliefs that a good manager is about to display something good which will increase sales volume.

This structure was widely accepted by subjects and proved to be quite stable. The third structure, on the other hand, led to the balanced but unhedonic conclusion that a disliked person, who is planning to do something unpleasant that will hurt sales, actually has injured sales in the past. When confronted with such a set of beliefs, consistent though they may be, subjects go on to add elaborations which will tend to maximize gain and minimize loss. They may, for example, in addition to accepting the communication making Fenwick completely negative, also accept the one which says he is really not going to go ahead with this plan to display modern art. Or the evaluation of modern art or its impact on sales may be made more positive. To sum up the findings of this experiment, then:

8. *In resolving cognitive discrepancies, subjects seek not only the attainment of balance and consistency but also the solution that maximizes potential gain and minimizes potential loss.* An analysis of the conditions under which one or the other will tend to prevail when the two forces are opposed awaits further experimentation.

In a last theoretical section Rosenberg and Abelson suggest a classification of underlying "microprocesses" which represent the assumed mediational events that may occur between encounters with cognitive imbalance and its reduction.

Changes in affect and belief following behavioral change

Brehm has replicated and extended the work of Festinger (1957) on dissonance theory. Specifically, he has investigated a special case of dissonance—that which arises from discrepant behavior, defined as the absence of, or the opposite of, behavior which is appropriate to the individual's affects and beliefs. A person who engages in such behavior is assumed to experience dissonance, a motivating condition that can

lead to his changing those affects and beliefs. The greater
the amount of dissonance, the greater the amount of change
likely to result: Brehm presents the following formula for
determining the magnitude of dissonance resulting from a
discrepant behavior:

$$\frac{\text{Dissonance from}}{\text{discrepant behavior}} = \frac{\text{Force against engaging in behavior}}{\text{Force for engaging in behavior}}$$

The forces for and against the behavior arise from the person's positive and/or negative attitudes toward the behavior
or object, and also from the contingencies of the situation—
e.g. the reward or punishment that will result from compliance or noncompliance. It is assumed that when dissonance
occurs, it is sometimes easier for the person to change his
affects and beliefs than it is for him to change his perceptions
of his own behavior or of physical reality.

A number of studies demonstrating that the expression
of arguments contrary to an individual's beliefs and feeling,
as in role-playing, tends to lead to their modification are
examined by Brehm. These studies do not make clear what
factors are responsible for the resulting changes. Is it necessary actually to engage in the persuasive behavior and be
rewarded for it, or is merely *deciding* to engage in discrepant
behavior sufficient to produce attitude change?

In order to examine the effects of nonpersuasive discrepant
behavior (behavior which does not involve repetition of facts
or arguments), children were induced by a reward to commit
themselves to eat varying amounts of a disliked vegetable. Information about individual preferences had been obtained
from a questionnaire administered three weeks earlier. Under
the guise of a "consumer research study," each student, seen
individually, was asked to fill out a questionnaire on the
vegetable he had said he disliked most, but which was presented to him by the experimenter as having been "randomly

chosen." He was asked to indicate his liking for the vegetable, and to estimate its vitamin content.

Next, each child was asked to eat some of the vegetable and was offered a prize for doing so. Commitment was varied in the following way: commitment to little eating (low-eat condition) was done by making the reward contingent on eating a single portion of the vegetable. Commitment to more eating (high-eat condition) was accomplished by making the reward contingent on eating a portion at the moment and also returning three or four times for more of it.

To vary the amount of cognitive support for engaging in the discrepant behavior, each subject was given, after eating, a "research report" on the food value of his vegetable. Some of the reports said that it was the best vegetable nutritionally; others said the vegetable was the worst. Finally, the subjects were asked to fill out the questionnaire on the vegetable again.

The results were that subjects in the high-eat condition showed less lowering of their vitamin estimate from the non-support communication, than did the low-eat and control subjects. These results confirm the prediction that:

9. *Commitment to a relatively great amount of discrepant behavior will increase resistance to belief of a nonsupporting communication and will increase acceptance of a supporting communication.*

Having demonstrated that engaging in persuasive behavior is not necessary to produce dissonance and subsequent attitude change, but that merely committing oneself to do something unpleasant is sufficient, Brehm goes on to ask: How necessary is the act of decision or commitment to the creation of dissonance? Will a discrepant event outside the individual's control lead to dissonance and hence motivate the person to change his attitude toward the event? To pursue this problem Brehm undertook to study the *fait accompli* situation in which an event occurs over which the individual has no control and which he would prevent if he could. The impact of a *fait accompli* was studied in an experiment similar to the vegetable-eating study described above. Some children were told, after eating, that their parents would receive a report informing them which vegetable the child had eaten. This implied to the subjects that they would then have to eat more of it at home. The result of this manpulation was a greater increase in liking for the vegetable in the *fait accompli* condition than in the control group.

In this experiment, although the subjects had no choice or prior knowledge about their parents being informed, they had actually made a choice just before the discrepant event— they had decided to sample the vegetable. To eliminate the prior choice factor, and to see if an unforeseen chance event could affect the magnitude of dissonance, another experiment was carried out by Brehm and Cohen (1959b).

All students in four undergraduate psychology classes were told they would have to participate in a long, tedious task —copying random numbers for three hours. There was great individual variation among subjects in the perceived ease with which they felt they could get out of this required participation. The data were therefore analyzed in terms of high and low perceived choice.

Each subject was informed that while most participants would be paid for the experiment, a few, chosen at random, would not be. Every subject was told he was one of those who, by chance, would not be paid. Some were told that the pay the others would be getting was $10, some were told it was $1. This manipulation was intended to vary relative deprivation.

The results showed that, for subjects who perceived little or no choice in regard to the unpleasant assignment, the greater the amount of relative deprivation, the lower their satisfaction with the assignment. On the other hand, for subjects who felt they did have a high degree of choice, the greater the relative deprivation, the higher their satisfaction with the assignment.

This experiment confirms the importance of subjective feelings of choice in the creation of dissonance, but since the relative deprivation was by "chance," the results also confirm the generalization that an event outside the individual's control can lead to dissonance and affect attitudes. Both this experiment and the one mentioned above support the proposition that:

10. *A disliked event outside the individual's control (a* fait accompli) *will result in positive change toward that event when the individual feels he could have avoided it or when he feels he did have prior choice.*

Further studies on the effects of choice are discussed by Brehm. An experiment by Cohen, Terry, and Jones (1959) showed that when subjects were given a choice as to whether to listen to material contrary to their own attitudes, those who felt they had high choice changed more in the direction of the communication. Also, the greater the discrepancy between the subject's initial position and the communication, the greater the attitude change. Brehm concludes that wherever there is a feeling of choice in relation to behavior discrepant with other attitude components, dissonance will be created and attitude change will tend to follow.

PROBLEMS FOR FURTHER RESEARCH

From the foregoing review of the main findings of the research reported in this volume it will be apparent that we are still some distance from the construction of a fully detailed theory of the interrelations between attitude components. But the results of the studies taken as a whole do suggest the directions which more comprehensive theoretical development might follow and indicate a number of important issues deserving of further investigation.

Four general problems seem to the authors particularly worthy of further research and theoretical analysis. The first of these is methodological and concerns the need for development of measures of degree of inconsistency between components of attitude. The second involves further analysis of the variables determining the individual's degree of reactivity to the presence of inconsistency. A third major problem concerns the nature of the motivational factors involved in maintaining consistency among attitude components. A last general problem involves analysis of the variables that exert influence upon the *type* of response made when inconsistency is introduced.

Measurement of degree of inconsistency

In the early stages of theorizing and research crude measurement of variables often suffices, but inevitably further progress can only be made when adequate scaling and evaluation of variables is provided. At the present time most theorists and researchers have to be satisfied with methods of measuring and manipulating inconsistency which take account only of its presence or absence. Future developments will undoubtedly require better measurement of degree of inconsistency.

Analogous problems are encountered in specifying similar terms, such as "degree of conflict," in conflict experiments. It is likely that we are dealing with the same basic phenomenon and may derive clues for measurement of inconsistency from the theorizing about factors affecting the degree of conflict. Research on conflict suggests that at least three factors should be distinguished: (1) the extent to which the responses made to the "conflict-inducing" stimulus patterns are incompatible (this shifts the problem to measurement of "response incompatibility"), (2) the extent to which the habit strengths of the two conflicting elements approach equality (Sears and Hovland, 1941), and (3) the absolute strengths of the two conflicting habits. When the two habits are of equal strength this last point is equivalent to the combined habit strength of the two components. Systematic research will be needed to develop adequate measures for what is equivalent to the "habit strength" of the stimulus-response connections for each of the response components in attitude as well as units in which to describe the degree of compatibility or incompatibility of the various responses.

Variables affecting degree of reactivity to inconsistency

In the studies reported in this volume the degree of inconsistency was not systematically varied, partly because of the lack of adequate measurement methods just discussed. Instead, types of inconsistency were introduced which would rank high on all three of the criteria discussed above. Even under conditions assumed to produce high inconsistency subjects vary considerably in their degree of response. They appear then to differ in the strength of their motivation to respond when confronted with inconsistency. In Chapter 2 it was postulated that such variation is coordinate with variation in an "intolerance-for-inconsistency threshold." For present purposes we are primarily concerned with response measures rather than with the intervening state of intolerance: thus we speak of a varying "threshold of response to inconsistency." However, at a number of points in this and later sections our analysis follows and elaborates upon the discussion in Chapter 2 of factors influencing the height of the intolerance-for-inconsistency threshold. Behind variation in responsiveness to inconsistency, then, are several important classes of variables.

Personality variables. A number of research studies have been reported in which the dependent variable of "general persuasability" is examined for its relation to patterns of variability in personality structure and content. Among these studies are the ones that were presented in the second volume of this series (Janis et al., 1959). A central finding that emerged from this group of studies is that a personality pattern characterized by low self-esteem and general passivity disposes the individual toward high persuasability.

One way of interpreting this finding is to argue that such persons will be insecure about the worth of their own knowledge and unsure of their own reasoning powers. Thus a previously stabilized attitude will be maintained at low levels of certainty and confidence. Such persons will also be more likely to "submit" to others who claim for themselves some status as authority or expert. It is the combination of these two related processes (i.e. low evaluation of oneself and one's powers and compensatory high evaluation of the powers of others claiming some special competence) which, according to a view set forth in the preceding volume, renders the individual so readily and generally persuasible.

A complementary explanation suggested by Cohen in the foregoing volume is advanced by the conceptual approaches represented by the studies reported in this volume. It is founded on the common clinical observation that a major defense against deep anxiety is the development and maintenance of one-sided, simply organized, unambiguous attitudes. Such attitudes may be useful to the highly anxious person because they impose superficial order and certainty upon areas of impulse and experience that are, in some deeper sense, chaotically disorganized. (A closely related interpretation is that offered by Adorno, Frenkel-Brunswik, and their co-workers, 1950, in connection with their demonstration that anxiety over repressed impulses is inversely correlated with "tolerance of ambiguity.")

This suggests that the type of neurotic person we have been describing will be disposed to handle his extreme anxieties by developing and expressing rigid, unambivalent attitudes. One might expect that such individuals would tend to reject inconsistency-arousing communications. However, because they lack confidence in the worth of their own knowledge and thought processes, they are comparatively incapable of rejecting such communications. Other responses, including general reorganization of attitude in directions influenced by inconsistency-arousing communications, will be more likely.

Further research based on these considerations might profitably attempt to measure the need for the maintenance of response consistency and to examine the correlation between the strength of this need, the degree of general neurotic anxiety, and responsiveness to inconsistency-producing communications.

Attitude-content variables. We have suggested above that certain types of personality may have characteristically low thresholds for responding to inconsistency between attitude components. It also seems clear from both everyday experience and experimental observation that for any given person some attitude constellations will be more resistant, and others less resistant, to alteration. Hovland, Harvey, and Sherif (1957) hold that the more intense or extreme the attitude in question, the more difficult it will be to produce change in that attitude. A possible explanation of this finding is suggested by the work of Smith, Bruner, and White (1956) and Sarnoff, Katz, and McClintock (1954)—the intensity of an attitude may in itself be closely correlated with the degree to which it reflects or symbolizes persisting motives of high intensity or, correspondingly, with the extent to which its expression offers some form of present need reduction or conflict resolution. This suggests the following hypothesis: The greater the extent to which the holding of a given attitude yields need reduction, the lower the threshold for response to inconsistency between the components of that attitude. However, in this case it would be expected that the most likely form of response would be re-establishment of the original attitude components and of the original relationship between them through rejection of the change that originally produced a suprathreshold degree of inconsistency.

It seems clear that the experimental investigation of this hypothesis could be undertaken if trustworthy methods for assessing the "functional value" of attitudes were available. If essentially similar attitudes were held by different persons who vary (either "naturally" or because of prior experimental treatment) in the amount of need reduction achieved through the attitude in question, it would be predicted that exposure to inconsistency-producing communications would produce widely different degrees of response.

Communicator and communication variables. Considerable research has been reported in which the production of attitude change is shown to be dependent both upon various attributes of the communicator who attempts to foster such change and upon certain aspects of the organization of his communications. In two previous volumes (Hovland, Janis, and Kelley, 1953; Hovland, et al., 1957) there were presented experiments along these lines that had been conducted by members of the Yale Communications Research Program.

It is possible to reinterpret these earlier findings in the light of our present analysis. Thus it may be hypothesized that the threshold for response to inconsistency between the components of an attitude will vary as a function, among many others, of the "credibility" of the communicator. Specifically, it may be predicted that the higher the communicator's perceived credibility (i.e. the greater the extent to which he is judged to be a trustworthy source of reliable information), the lower the threshold for response to inconsistency aroused by his communications.

Similarly we may re-examine the implications of the finding reported earlier (Hovland et al., 1957) that "when contradictory information is presented in a *single communication* by a *single communicator,* there is a pronounced tendency for those items presented first to dominate the impression received." An extrapolative implication of this finding is that in this situation the structure of the communication operates to set the threshold for response to inconsistency at a higher level than would be the case if *two different communicators* presented the two separate and mutually inconsistent portions of the contradictory information. Along the same lines it may be hypothesized that even when a single communicator presents contradictory messages, if he were to present them in two distinct portions separated by some extraneous intervening activity the threshold for response to inconsistency would be somewhat lower than if they were presented as parts of a "single" communication. This is in accord with the empirical results reported in the foregoing volume.

Still another possibility is that certain kinds of communication *content* may affect the height of the threshold for response to inconsistency. We have in mind specifically the possibility that attitude change attempts featuring communications designed to arouse inconsistency may be preceded by communications which in themselves are intended to lower the threshold for response to such inconsistency. Such communications might for example stress the desirability of consistency as such or they might suggest that acceptance of inconsistency is a mark of "intellectual laziness" or of "irrationality." Basic to this hypothesis is the systematic assumption that the threshold value characteristic of a given point in time is a function of the degree of arousal of motivational forces at that same point in time. Increase in the degree of arousal of such motivational forces should result in decrease in the threshold for response to inconsistency between attitude components.

Situational variables. The same individual may be more responsive to the presence of inconsistency under one set of circumstances than another. Thus there is a situational factor to be considered. It may be predicted that when a person is publicly expressing his attitudinal responses he will be more concerned with the maintenance and defense of consistency between different attitude components than when he is engaging in private, unshared processes of symbolic activity. Similarly, not all situations in which one discloses one's attitudes and thought processes are equal in the extent to which they are guided by consensual standards in favor of consistency and integration between related response components; considerably more consistency is expected and sought in the meeting of a college debating society than in an intimate dialogue between lovers.

From these considerations there emerge two related hypotheses which need research investigation. The first of these is simply that the more public and visible the individual's expression of his attitudes, the lower the threshold of reactivity to inconsistency. The second hypothesis is that the greater the social goal of consistency (or more generally of "rationality") aroused by the situation, the lower the threshold for response to inconsistency.

It will be noted that although McGuire and Rosenberg and Abelson in their respective chapters assume the validity of the first of these two hypotheses, it has not been put to the test. If, as we would expect, both the first and the second hypotheses are empirically established it will be desirable to examine their dynamic or mediational bases. For example, it might be asked of the relationship posited in the first hypothesis whether it is due to a widely shared social expectation that one is judged positively by others when showing consistency and negatively when showing inconsistency. Or it could be maintained that in a public situation one cannot readily deal with inconsistency by withdrawing attention from it: thus the person may be more vigilant toward inconsistency of small magnitude in public situations than in private ones.

An interesting question may be raised as to whether the effects demonstrated in the present studies may not in some part reflect a striving toward consistency which might be due primarily to the subject's unvoiced apprehensions and anticipations about the "rules of the game" when participating in experiments and dealing with experimenters. In its most radical form this question could be asked: Is it not possible that in real life people do not particularly value consistency between response components and that they do not really strive to achieve or conserve it? In other words, it may be contended that our conceptualization of a response threshold is not applicable outside the realm of attitude experiments. Stated in so extreme a form this objection seems to violate the vast accumulation of evidence from the sphere of daily experience. Yet it draws attention to the possibility that the demands of the situation in which consistency itself is being subjected to research study may differ considerably from those of other situations in which inconsistency between attitude components can be aroused and experienced.

The nature of mediating processes

The stress in the present work has been upon experimental evaluations of various hypotheses concerning relationships between independent and dependent variables. But the class of topics which we have just been discussing, as well as others considered throughout earlier chapters, raises questions as to the nature of the processes which mediate the changes in relationships between components when inconsistency between them is introduced. One type of theorizing about intervening variables or mediating processes is found in the chapter by Rosenberg and Abelson in their section concerned with a "microprocess analysis of cognitive balancing." Here they consider a reductionist analysis of the minute details of the symbolic processes through which cognitive, affective, and behavioral responses become altered. An entire program of research lies implicit in their discussion of these processes.

A central problem in the analysis of mediating processes, and one which has concerned most of our predecessors, is that of motivation. Sumner (1907) invokes a motive which he calls the "strain toward consistency." Lund (1925) speaks of the "need for consistency." Newcomb (1953) conceptualizes a "strain toward symmetry." Festinger regards dissonance (created by inconsistency between cognitions) as having motivelike properties (similar, he says, to hunger and thirst).

The question of "consciousness" is implicit in any theorizing about motives. Festinger makes no assumption about whether the organism consciously "experiences" dissonance, although at one point he does speak of a subject's "having learned, during the course of his existence, how unpleasant dissonance is" (p. 268). The whole problem of whether responsiveness to inconsistency requires awareness seems to be an open one. It is often convenient to speak in these terms since in attitude studies we are primarily concerned with processes which are conscious and capable of verbalization and articulation. But at the same time we must recognize that other writers find it important to stress the extent to which attitudes are derivative from, and indirectly reductive of, unconscious conflicts and motivations (see e.g. Smith, Bruner, and White, 1956; Sarnoff, Katz, and McClintock, 1954). Similarly, psychoanalytically oriented personality theories clearly assume that patterns of response inconsistency of which the person is quite unaware (i.e. repressed, unconscious conflicts) are motivating: they generate behavioral attempts at inconsistency reduction. We do not see at present any clear-cut way of testing the differential implications of these alternative formulations.

There are at least three important formulations on the origin and functioning of the motivation to maintain interresponse consistency. One of these, derived from Gestalt formulations of perception, is that of Krech and Crutchfield (1948). For them the person's tendency to maintain consistency within a complex attitude is a reflection of a general striving toward organized patterning of related elements. It is then a specific case of the widely operative motivation toward the elaboration and stabilization of ordered forms. While they do not rule out the possibility that this type of basic motivation may be influenced and heightened by experience factors, Krech and Crutchfield seem willing to accept the conventional Gestalt psychology emphasis on unlearned, autochthonous determination.

A second approach stresses the learned aspect of response to inconsistency by highlighting one major type of early experience. Theorists of this stripe argue that from his first days the human individual encounters both positive and negative reinforcements in connection with a large number of specific environmental "objects." One consequence is that by virtue of his double-valued orientation toward certain objects he cannot approach them to the degree that enables consummatory activity and need reduction. Nor can he readily disregard these objects or move so far away from them as to enable easy redirection of his approach orientation. Being caught in conflict is frustrating in still another sense: not only does it produce frustration through delay of gratification of the motives involved but it tends to generate an extra quantity of tension associated with the experience of conflict as such.

Ignoring details of analysis and terminology we find a general consensus among those who have described and studied this common form of conflict that it is a highly motivating situation—one that arouses behavioral measures whose ultimate effect is a reorganization that makes possible direct access to previously blocked goal states and thus also makes possible the reduction or elimination of the special tension caused by being in conflict.

Among the many behavioral expedients available to animals in conflict, one that seems virtually unique to man is symbolic manipulation. He far more than any other animal can change his ideational representations of the objects of the environment relevant to his conflict; probably he only can maintain a dialogue with himself in which he is capable of altering his ways of representing what he feels, believes, and intends toward the conflict-relevant objects. Indeed it may be argued that a good part of what in psychoanalytic parlance is meant by the "ego" and by "ego skills" is based upon the acquisition and exercise of these special abilities during the early years of life.

With these considerations in mind we may note the simple point that a socialized human, by the time he has come to maturity, will have undergone thousands of "training trials" in which "conflict-like" situations have been altered, and their attendant frustrations reduced or eliminated, through active efforts at reorganizing the representation of certain aspects or components of those situations so as to reduce the inconsistency between them. When the total representation of a conflict-arousing situation has been so transformed that its objects do not elicit competing and incompatible response tendencies, the conflict has been solved; overt behavior productive of need reduction has become possible and is undertaken and carried to completion.

The long-term consequence of an extended history of such transactions repeated again and again will be that the state of "consistency" between affective, cognitive, and overt behavioral responses toward objects will become, in itself, a desired and gratifying state of affairs; it will have the status of a basic learned incentive. And of course from this it follows that the encounter with extensive inconsistency between such responses (even when they do not correspond to an active and ongoing "conflict" in the technical sense) will be psychologically painful and will activate the individual's learned skills of response reorganization.

The third formulation of the origin and functioning of a mediating response to inconsistency involves the assumption that it is a product of direct and deliberate social training. It is argued that in all known groups there exists some form of consensual standard calling for the sort of consistency with which we are here concerned. To be sure, few social or cultural settings impose this demand so strongly or exhaustively as do such special subcultures as the court of law or the philosophy seminar; usually, however, persons will encounter *some* negative evaluations of themselves or of their communications when those communications are grossly and internally inconsistent.

We may explicate our point by some comments on the patterning of the individual's early social experience. Parents and other adults engaged in significant interaction with children will in the course of a child's development sooner or later begin to evaluate some of his verbal productions in the light of the consensual standard favoring response consistency. They will sometimes, and probably with increasing frequency, judge the child's ideational-affective performance as poor when it contains large inconsistencies; they will elicit response reorganization in the direction of consistency ("But, darling, how can you say you hate nursery school when you say you like the children and the finger-painting and the crackers and milk?"). Clearly such normative evaluations communicated in many interactional sequences over a number of years will operate, through well known "laws of learning," to generate an habitual striving toward the maintenance of consistency and the reduction of gross inconsistency. At the same time it is apparent that in certain kinds of social groups, such as those concerned with the artistic elaboration of human experience or with the mystical investigation of its enigmas, the converse norm often applies: consistency is condemned as "the hobgoblin of small minds." But even in such special environments routine aspects of communication seem often to be governed by the normative expectation that feelings, percepts, and overt acts will be integrated with one another.

Either of the two theoretical approaches that we have reviewed could encompass and explain the assertion that consistency norms are available in all cultures. If the motivation toward consistency is universally distributed across all members of the species (whether this motivation is due to processes that do or do not involve the conditioning effects of social experience) it would follow that some parallel normative representation of this motivation would be developed wherever groups of humans have organized or "inherited" a social system. We suggest then that the motivation toward consistency is not only a product of consistency norms but also a factor disposing toward the elaboration and stabilization of such norms. This kind of circular pattern, in which social standards both reflect and maintain individual needs, has been described and analyzed by the functional school of anthropology.

We have, to this point in our analysis, presented three

broad lines of interpretation on how it happens that people are motivated to reject and reduce inconsistency between related responses. Definitive evidence enabling the rejection of any one of these viewpoints is not available. The authors, however, find the second of the three theoretical approaches most congenial and believe that it best delineates the major source of the motivation toward the achievement and maintenance of consistency between related responses. At the same time the contribution of normative standards to the development of consistency motivation (as described in the last of the three theoretical approaches reviewed here) must be acknowledged. It remains for further research to "apportion the variance" attributable to each of the separate sources and to their interaction.

Alternative responses to inconsistency

The principal type of response to inconsistency with which the present volume has been concerned has been change in one or another of the components of attitude so as to produce reorganization and reorientation in that attitude (i.e. "attitude change"). This is a frequent type of response to the presence of inconsistency, but it is by no means the only one. Thus Brehm in Chapter 5 reports evidence that the performance of an act inconsistent with one's affect and cognition does not necessarily produce changes in the affective and cognitive components. In terms of "dissonance" analysis this situation may be handled not only by changing one's affect toward the performance in question but also by "enhancing the negative consequences that would have occurred if he had not complied" or by "changing the apparent rewards to be gained by compliance." Both of these alternatives do permit some reduction of "dissonance."

Similarly Rosenberg suggests a number of outcomes in which inconsistency is reduced by methods other than changes leading to general reorganization of attitude. One of these is simply the ultimate rejection of the inconsistency-arousing communication. By this expedient the person achieves consistency restoration by the reestablishment of the original attitude whose inner organization was temporarily disrupted by a communication designed to produce attitude change. He suggests too that under other circumstances, where the force of the communications operating on the person is such that they cannot be fully rejected, the individual may employ certain repressionlike devices which effectively isolate the inconsistent components from one another and thus enable him to avoid reorganizing his attitude in the direction required by those communications.

When a large number of different types of responses may be made to any particular manifestation of inconsistency one must be most rigorous in specifying in complete detail the factors that will determine which particular response will be made. Otherwise we have the situation frequently encountered in theorizing where one can explain the failure to obtain a predicted outcome as attributable to the subject's responding in other ways delineated in the theory but not measured in the experiment. Accordingly it is an important future research task to spell out in systematic detail the conditions under which one or another type of consistency-reestablishing response is made to the presence of inconsistency.

In experiments of this type and in related ones by Festinger and his colleagues the design usually involves setting up conditions that block off other kinds of response so that changes in the components of attitude are highlighted. For other purposes one might proceed with an entirely different strategy and allow other types of response to be dominant. Two hypotheses which merit testing are suggested. The first is that, except in the case of general lack of self-esteem, the lower the person's threshold of response to inconsistency the more likely it is that he will respond in ways other than reorganizing the attitude through changing the inconsistent attitude components. This is based on the assumption that a lower threshold of reactivity to inconsistency represents a greater degree of motivation to defend and maintain a consistent organization of related response components. Where this is a major motivation, consistency may be sought with maximal speed and with minimal over-all reorganization of the other components of attitude. Rejecting the inconsistency-arousing communication is, in this sense, the most efficient and least costly adaptation and might be expected to be the most likely outcome. (However, as has been noted, if rejection of the communication is blocked off, such a person would be expected to show a large degree of change.)

A second hypothesis is that the less the degree to which situational constraints force the individual to attend to and examine the temporary inconsistency, the greater the likelihood that he will handle it by withdrawing attention, i.e. by "stopping thought." At the same time we may hypothesize that "stopping thought" will be less available as an alternative to the degree that the attitude is ego-central (i.e. is focused on some "object" of high motivational significance).

The foregoing comments describe some types of response to attitude inconsistency which are available alternatives to attitude reorganization when the person is motivated to *reduce* inconsistency. However, our discussion of responses to inconsistency would be incomplete if it neglected to note that there are certain settings in which, and certain persons in whom, motives favoring the *arousal and maintenance* of inconsistency are sometimes dominant.

Thus in an earlier comment we noted that the search for and achievement of "consistency" is not always accepted as a legitimate imperative. We noted particularly that in certain approaches to life, or in certain groups which elaborate and celebrate such approaches, inconsistency and paradox may be actively sought as the pathway to "higher truths." However, close perusal of the affectively toned ideational processes of artists and "mystics" suggests that the arousal and expansion of inconsistency often operates as a mediational process or instrumental sequence culminating in the achievement of some higher integration, some new ideational formula or invention, through which seemingly divergent and incompatible responses are brought into balance. Certainly a good deal of "scientific thinking" seems to feature this same sort of sequence. The scientist by his training is set to attend to the disconfirming case, to avoid premature closure: but always in the hope that ultimately a higher and more veridical interpretation will thereby become available.

Returning to our primary concern with social attitudes, we should note that, while they have not particularly addressed themselves to the possibility that men are sometimes motivated to seek paradox and destroy consistency, both McGuire in his chapter and Rosenberg and Abelson in theirs have felt compelled by their data to call attention to certain kinds of motivation which exert counter-consistency influence upon the symbolic and overt behaviors undertaken by persons responding to inconsistency. Thus McGuire conceptualizes a tendency toward "wish fulfillment" as sometimes operating in opposition to forces driving the person to the achievement of full consistency between related attitudinal beliefs (or, in his terms, "logical thinking"). Similarly, Rosenberg and Abelson interpret a portion of their data as indicating that the motivation toward achieving "balance" within structures of "attitudinal cognition" is sometimes countermanded by a "hedonic tendency": i.e. a striving toward the maximization of potential gain and minimization of potential loss ("gain" and "loss" refer simply to the fulfillment or violation of the person's major regnant motives).

Our understanding of such anticonsistency processes is extremely rudimentary. Indeed we are yet some distance from the achievement of a classification scheme for the various effects that feature abandonment or subordination of the motivation toward consistency. At present we can do little more to advance understanding of this problem than note a few other phenomena which highlight it.

For example, it is worth noting that there are some kinds of choice phenomena that seem to involve an increase rather than a reduction in incompatibility through the apparent enhancement of the unchosen rather than the chosen alternative. This is in contrast to the experiments reported in this volume by Brehm and to the theorizing of Festinger on "dissonance," which stress the likelihood of an increase over time in the preference for the chosen alternative. Reduced liking for the unchosen alternative is an important effect and is characterized popularly in terms of "sour grapes." But the opposing phenomenon is also frequently seen and undoubtedly deserves research attention. We have in mind situations in which the unchosen alternative becomes enhanced in recollection as compared with the chosen alternative. This outcome may be seen as a manifestation of the proverb which proclaims that "grass looks greener in the neighbor's yard."

Illustrative of this category is the report that refugee groups at the time of emigrating have a low opinion of the country they are leaving and see all of its defects. After a stay in a camp for displaced persons for a number of years, however, they are said to become nostalgic and to exaggerate the attractiveness of the country they have left. This serves to increase rather than reduce the discrepancy between the chosen and unchosen alternative. Similarly in a recent study it was found that attitudes of Air Force lieutenants who had left the service increased in favorableness toward the Air Force over time (Kerckhoff, ed., 1958).

Undoubtedly the conditions that intervene between the making of a decision and the postdecision evaluation play an important part. But it is also likely that adequate analysis will require a more sophisticated classification of predecision choices to clarify the differential conditions for one or the other mode of resolution. A major problem to which future research must be addressed is to determine the conditions under which motivational processes directing the person away from the goal of consistency are aroused and maintained.

REFERENCES

Italic numbers at the end of each reference refer to pages in the present volume.

ABELSON, R. P., 1959. Modes of resolution of belief dilemmas. *Conflict Resolution, 3*, 343–52. *152*

ABELSON, R. P. and ROSENBERG, M. J., 1958. Symbolic psycho-logic: a model of attitudinal cognition. *Behav. Sci., 3*, 1–13. *5, 13, 60, 65, 72f., 117, 120f., 160f.*

ADORNO, T. W., FRENKEL-BRUNSWIK, ELSE, LEVINSON, D. J., and SANFORD, R. N., 1950. *The authoritarian personality.* New York, Harper. *7, 52, 216f.*

ARONSON, E. and MILLS, J., 1959. The effect of severity of initiation on liking for a group. *J. Abnorm. Soc. Psychol., 59*, 177–81. *183f.*

ASCH, S. E., 1940. Studies in the principles of judgments and attitudes: II. Determination of judgments by group and ego standards. *J. Soc. Psychol., 12*, 433–65. *34, 155, 158*

ASCH, S. E., BLOCK, HELEN, and HERTZMAN, M., 1938. Studies in the principles of judgments and attitudes: I. Two basic principles of judgment. *J. Psychol., 5*, 219–51. *96*

AXELROD, J., 1959. *The relationship of mood and of mood shift to attitude.* Technical Report No. 5 to the Office of Naval Research (mimeographed). University of Rochester. *5*

BERELSON, B. R., LAZARSFELD, P. F., and MCPHEE, W. N., 1954. *Voting: a study of opinion formation in a presidential campaign.* Chicago, University of Chicago Press. *71*

BIRCH, H. G., 1945. The effect of socially disapproved labeling upon a well-structured attitude. *J. Abnorm. Soc. Psychol., 40*, 301–10. *96*

BLAU, P., 1953. Orientation of college students toward international relations. *Amer. J. Sociol., 59*, 205–14. *71*

BREHM, J. W., 1956. Postdecision changes in the desirability of alternatives. *J. Abnorm. Soc. Psychol., 52*, 384–9. *186*

BREHM, J. W., 1959. Increasing cognitive dissonance by a *fait accompli. J. Abnorm. Soc. Psychol., 58*, 379–82. *187ff.*

BREHM, J. W., 1960. Attitudinal consequences of commitment to unpleasant behavior. *J. Abnorm. Soc. Psychol., 60*, 379–83. *174f.*

BREHM, J. W. and COHEN, A. R., 1959a. Re-evaluation of choice alternatives as a function of their number and qualitative similarity. *J. Abnorm. Soc. Psychol., 58*, 373–8. *186*

233

BREHM, J. W. and COHEN, A. R., 1959b. Choice and chance relative deprivation as determinants of cognitive dissonance. *J. Abnorm. Soc. Psychol.*, *58*, 383–7. *189ff., 194f., 212f.*

BRIM, O. G., 1955. Attitude content-intensity and probability expectations. *Amer. Soc. Rev.*, *20*, 68–76. *97*

BROCK, T. C., and SEARS, D. O., 1960. The effects of cognitive organization on acceptance of discrepant information. Unpublished paper, Yale University. *161*

BURDICK, H. A. and BURNES, A. J., 1958. A test of "strain toward symmetry" theories. *J. Abnorm. Soc. Psychol.*, *57*, 367–70. *9*

CANTRIL, H., 1938. The prediction of social events. *J. Abnorm. Soc. Psychol.*, *33*, 364–89. *66*

CARLSON, E. R., 1956. Attitude change through modification of attitude structure. *J. Abnorm. Soc. Psychol.*, *52*, 256–61. *5, 10, 24, 51*

CARTWRIGHT, D., 1949. Some principles of mass persuasion. *Human Relat.*, *2*, 253–67. *6, 16f., 51*

CARTWRIGHT, D. and HARARY, F., 1956. Structural balance: a generalization of Heider's theory. *Psychol. Rev.*, *63*, 277–93. *5, 17, 60, 65, 72f., 115*

CHEIN, I., 1948. Behavior theory and the behavior of attitudes. *Psychol. Rev.*, *55*, 175–88. *16*

COCHRAN, W. G. and COX, GERTRUDE M., 1950. *Experimental designs*. New York, Wiley. *132*

COHEN, A. R., BREHM, J. W., and FLEMING, W. H., 1958. Attitude change and justification for compliance. *J. Abnorm. Soc. Psychol.*, *56*, 276–8. *171f.*

COHEN, A. R., TERRY, H. I., and JONES, C. B., 1959. Attitudinal effects of choice in exposure to counter-propaganda. *J. Abnorm. Soc. Psychol.*, *58*, 388–91. *192f., 213*

COOMBS, C. H., 1952. A theory of psychological scaling. *Univ. of Mich. Engng. Res. Bull. No. 34*, Ann Arbor, University of Michigan Press. *26*

COOPER, EUNICE and DINERMAN, HELEN, 1951. Analysis of the film "Don't Be a Sucker": a study in communication. *Publ. Opin. Quart.*, *15*, 243–64. *91*

CRONBACH, L. J., 1946. Response sets and test validity. *Educ. Psychol. Measmt.*, *6*, 475–94. *96*

CRONBACH, L. J., 1950. Further evidence of response sets and test design. *Educ. Psychol. Measmt.*, *10*, 3–31. *96*

DEUTCH, M. and SOLOMON, L., 1959. Reactions to evaluations by others as influenced by self-evaluations. *Sociometry*, *22*, 93–112. *146*

DOOB, L. W., 1948. *Public opinion and propaganda*. New York, Holt. *23*

FESTINGER, L., 1954. A theory of social comparison processes. *Human Relat.*, *7*, 117–40. *146*

FESTINGER, L., 1957. *A theory of cognitive dissonance*. Evanston, Row, Peterson. *9, 66, 70, 86, 116, 147, 162, 164ff., 186, 193f., 209, 222*

FESTINGER, L. and CARLSMITH, J. M., 1959. Cognitive consequences of forced compliance. *J. Abnorm. Soc. Psychol.*, *58*, 203–10. *172f.*

FRENCH, V. V., 1947. The structure of sentiments. *J. Pers.*, *15*, 247–282. *16*

GREEN, B. F., 1954. Attitude measurement. In *Handbook of social psychology*, Vol. 1, ed. G. Lindzey. Cambridge, Mass., Addison-Wesley, 335–69. *5*

GREEN, R. F., GUILFORD, J. P., CHRISTENSEN, R. P., and COMREY, A. L., 1953. A factor analytic study of reasoning abilities. *Psychometrika*, *18*, 135–160. *71*

GUILFORD, J. P., COMREY, A. L., GREEN, R. F., and CHRISTENSEN, R. P., 1950. *A factor analytic study of reasoning ability. I. Hypotheses and discussion of tests*. Report No. 1. Los Angeles, University of Southern California. *71*

GUILFORD, J. P., COMREY, A. L., GREEN, R. F., and CHRISTENSEN, R. P., 1951. *A factor analytic study of reasoning ability. II. Administering of tests and analyses of results*. Report No. 3. Los Angeles, University of Southern California. *See also* Reports Nos. 6, 7, and 9. *71*

HARARY, F., 1959. On measurement of structural balance. *Behav. Sci.*, *4*, 316–23. *121, 146*

HARDING, J., KUTNER, B., PROSHANSKY, H., and CHEIN, I., 1954. Prejudice and ethnic relations. In *Handbook of social psychology*, Vol. 2, ed. G. Lindzey. Cambridge, Mass., Addison-Wesley, 1021–61. *4f., 23*

HARTLEY, E. L., 1946. *Problems in prejudice*. New York, King's Crown Press. *5*

HEIDER, F., 1946. Attitudes and cognitive organization. *J. Psychol.*, *21*, 107–12. *5, 9, 16, 60, 65, 73, 113*

HEIDER, F., 1958. *The psychology of interpersonal relations*. New York, Wiley. *9, 60, 65, 73, 113ff., 118, 146*

HILLIARD, A. L., 1950. *The forms of value*. New York, Columbia University Press. *16*

HOROWITZ, M. W., LYONS, J., and PERLMUTTER, H. V., 1951. Induction of forces in discussion groups. *Human Relat.*, *4*, 57–76. *9, 115*

HOVLAND, C. I., 1954. Effects of the mass media of communication. In *Handbook of social psychology*, Vol. 2, ed. G. Lindzey. Cambridge, Mass., Addison-Wesley, 1062–103. *5, 23*

HOVLAND, C. I., HARVEY, O. J., and SHERIF, M., 1957. Assimilation and contrast effects in reactions to communication and attitude change. *J. Abnorm. Soc. Psychol.*, *55*, 244–52. *54, 97, 217, 219*

HOVLAND, C. I., JANIS, I. L., and KELLEY, H. H., 1953. *Communication and persuasion*. New Haven, Yale University Press. *218*

HOVLAND, C. I., LUMSDAINE, A. A., and SHEFFIELD, F. D., 1949. *Experiments on mass communication*. Princeton, Princeton University Press. *71, 91*

HOVLAND, C. I. and MANDELL, W., 1952. An experimental comparison of conclusion-drawing by the communicator and by the audience. *J. Abnorm. Soc. Psychol.*, *47*, 581–8. *91f.*

HOVLAND, C. I., MANDELL, W., CAMPBELL, ENID H., BROCK, T., LUCHINS, A. S., COHEN, A. R., McGUIRE, W. J., JANIS, I. L., FEIERABEND, ROSALIND L., and ANDERSON, N. H., 1957. *The order of presentation in persuasion*. New Haven, Yale University Press. *2, 4, 54, 218f.*

HOVLAND, C. I. and WEISS, W., 1951. The influence of source credibility on communication effectiveness. *Publ. Opin. Quart.*, *15*, 635–50. *96*

JANIS, I. L., HOVLAND, C. I., FIELD, P. B., LINTON, HARRIET, GRAHAM, ELAINE, COHEN, A. R., RIFE, D., ABELSON, R. P., LESSER, G. S., and KING, B. T., 1959. *Personality and persuasibility*. New Haven, Yale University Press. *4, 54, 216*

JANIS, I. L. and KING, B. T., 1954. The influence of role playing on opinion change. *J. Abnorm. Soc. Psychol.*, *49*, 211–18. *170*

JORDAN, N., 1953. Behavioral forces that are a function of attitudes and of cognitive organization. *Human Relat.*, *6*, 273–87. *9, 114*

KATZ, D. and BRALY, K., 1933. Racial stereotypes of one-hundred college students. *J. Abnorm. Soc. Psychol.*, *28*, 280–90. *4*

KATZ, D. and KAHN, R. L., 1952. Some recent findings in human-relations research in industry. In *Readings in social psychology*, eds. G. E. Swanson, T. M. Newcomb, and E. L. Hartley. New York, Holt. 650–65. *6*

KATZ, D. and STOTLAND, E., 1959. A preliminary statement to a theory of attitude structure and change. In *Psychology: a study of a science*, Vol. 3, ed. S. Koch. New York, McGraw Hill, 423–75. *3, 5*

KELLEY, H. H., 1955. Salience of membership and resistance to change of group-anchored attitudes. *Human Relat.*, *8*, 275–89. *96*

✓ KELMAN, H. C., 1953. Attitude change as a function of response restriction. *Human Relat.*, *6*, 185–214. *70f., 169f.*

KERCKHOFF, A. C. (ed.), 1958. *The reactions of a group of former Air Force lieutenants to two years of civilian life*. Technical Report, Air Force Personnel and Trng. Res. Center, Lackland Air Force Base, Texas, ASTIA Document No. AD152-126. *232*

KING, B. T. and JANIS, I. L., 1956. Comparison of the effectiveness of improvised versus non-improvised role-playing in producing opinion changes. *Human Relat.*, *9*, 177–86. *170f.*

KOGAN, N. and TAGIURI, R., 1958. Interpersonal preference and cognitive organization. *J. Abnorm. Soc. Psychol.*, *56*, 113–16. *9, 115*

KRAMER, B. M., 1949. Dimensions of prejudice. *J. Psychol.*, *27*, 389–451. *5*

KRECH, D. and CRUTCHFIELD, R., 1948. *Theory and problems of social psychology*. New York, McGraw-Hill. *5, 15f., 223*

✓ LAPIERE, R. T., 1934. Attitudes versus actions. *Soc. Forc.*, *13*, 230–7. *6*

✓ LAWSON, E. D. and STAGNER, R., 1957. Group pressure, attitude change, and autonomic involvement. *J. Soc. Psychol.*, *45*, 299–312. *3*

LAZARSFELD, P. F., BERELSON, B., and GAUDET, HAZEL, 1944. *The people's choice*. New York, Duell, Sloan and Pearce. *7*

LAZARUS, R. S. and MCLEARY, R. A., 1951. Autonomic discrimination without awareness: a study of subception. *Psychol. Rev.*, *58*, 113–22. *6*

LEFFORD, A., 1946. The influence of emotional subject matter on logical reasoning. *J. Gen. Psychol.*, *34*, 127–51. *99*

LINDQUIST, E. F., 1953. *Design and analysis of experiments in psychology and education*. Boston, Houghton Mifflin. *132*

LORGE, I., 1937. Gen-like: halo or reality. *Psychol. Bull.*, *34*, 545–6. *97*

LUND, F. H., 1925. The psychology of belief. *J. Abnorm. Soc. Psychol.*, *20*, 63–81; 174–96. *7, 66, 222*

MATHEWS, C. O., 1927. The effect of position of printed response words upon children's answers to questions in two-response types of tests. *J. Ed. Psychol.*, *18*, 445–57. *97*

McDOUGALL, W., 1908. *An introduction to social psychology.* London, Methuen. *3*

McGREGOR, D., 1938. The major determinants of the prediction of social events. *J. Abnorm. Soc. Psychol.*, *33*, 179–204. *66*

MERTON, R. K. and KITT, ALICE S., 1950. Contributions to the theory of reference group behavior. In *Studies in the scope and method of "The American Soldier,"* eds. R. K. Merton and P. F. Lazarsfeld. Glencoe, Free Press. *189, 191*

MILLS, J., 1958. Changes in moral attitudes following temptation. *J. Pers. 26*, 517–31. *182f.*

MOORE, H. T., 1921. The comparative influence of majority and expert opinion. *Am. J. Psychol.*, *32*, 16–20. *96*

MORGAN, J. J. B. and MORTON, J. T., 1944. The distortion of syllogistic reasoning produced by personal convictions. *J. Soc. Psychol.*, *20*, 39–59. *100*

MORGAN, W. J. and MORGAN, ANTONIA B., 1953. Logical reasoning: with and without training. *J. Appl. Psychol.*, *37*, 399–406. *71*

MORISSETTE, J. O., 1958. An experimental study of the theory of structural balance. *Human Relat.*, *11*, 239–54. *115, 120*

MOSTELLER, F. and BUSH, R. R., 1954. Selected quantitative techniques. In *Handbook of social psychology*, Vol. 1, ed. G. Lindzey. Cambridge, Mass., Addison-Wesley, 289–334. *29*

MURPHY, G., MURPHY, LOIS B., and NEWCOMB, T. M., 1937. *Experimental social psychology.* New York, Harper. *7, 23*

MURRAY, H. A., et al., 1938. *Explorations in personality.* New York, Oxford University Press. *19*

MURRAY, H. A. and MORGAN, CHRISTIANA D., 1945. A clinical study of sentiments. *Genet. Psychol. Monogr.*, *32*, 3–311. *7*

MYRDAL, G., 1944. *An American Dilemma.* New York, Harper. *98*

NEWCOMB, T. M., 1943. *Personality and social change.* New York, Dryden. *7*

NEWCOMB, T. M., 1953. An approach to the study of communicative acts. *Psychol. Rev.*, *60*, 393–404. *9, 60, 65, 73, 115f., 222*

NEWCOMB, T. M., 1958. The cognition of persons as cognizers. In *Person perception and interpersonal behavior*, eds. R. Tagiuri and L. Petrullo. Stanford, Stanford University Press, 179–90. *115*

NEWCOMB, T. M., 1959. Individual systems of orientation. In *Psychology: a study of a science*, Vol. 3, ed. S. Koch. New York, McGraw-Hill, 384–422. *9, 116*

NEWELL, A., SHAW, J. C., and SIMON, H. A., 1959. *Report on a general problem solving program*. Rand Corporation Report P1584 (mimeographed). Santa Monica, California. *160, 162*

NOWLIS, V., 1960. *Some studies of the influence of films on mood and attitude*. Technical Report No. 7 to the Office of Naval Research (mimeographed). University of Rochester. *5*

O'CONNOR, PATRICIA, 1952. Ethnocentrism, "intolerance of ambiguity," and abstract reasoning ability. *J. Abnorm. Soc. Psychol., 47,* 526–30. *98*

OSGOOD, C. E., 1960. Cognitive dynamics in the conduct of human affairs. *Publ. Opin. Quart., 24,* 341–65. *151*

OSGOOD, C. E., SAPORTA, S., and NUNNALLY, J. C., 1956. Evaluative assertion analysis. *Litera, 3,* 47–102. *72, 118*

OSGOOD, C. E., SUCI, G. J., and TANNENBAUM, P. H., 1958. *The measurement of meaning*. Urbana, University of Illinois Press. *5, 149*

OSGOOD, C. E., and TANNENBAUM, P. H., 1955. The principle of congruity in the prediction of attitude change. *Psychol. Rev., 62,* 42–55. *9, 60, 65, 72, 96f., 116, 149ff., 160*

PEAK, HELEN, 1955. Attitude and motivation. In *Nebraska symposium on motivation*, ed. M. R. Jones. Lincoln, University of Nebraska Press, 149–88. *16*

PEAK, HELEN, 1958. Psychological structure and psychological activity. *Psychol. Rev., 65,* 325–47. *5*

PEAK, HELEN, 1959. *The effects of aroused motivation on attitudes*. Technical Report No. 8 to the Office of Naval Research (mimeographed). Ann Arbor, University of Michigan. *5, 10, 24, 51*

RABBIE, J. M., BREHM, J. W., and COHEN, A. R., 1959. Verbalization and reactions to cognitive dissonance. *J. Pers., 27,* 407–17. *186f.*

REITMAN, W. R., 1959. Heuristic programs, computer simulation, and higher mental processes. *Behav. Sci., 4,* 330–5. *163*

ROSENBERG, M. J., 1953. The experimental investigation of a value theory of attitude structure. Unpublished doctoral dissertation, University of Michigan. *11, 17ff.*

ROSENBERG, M. J., 1956. Cognitive structure and attitudinal affect. *J. Abnorm. Soc. Psychol., 53,* 367–72. *5, 11, 17ff.*

ROSENBERG, M. J., 1960. Cognitive reorganization in response to the hypnotic reversal of attitudinal affect. *J. Pers., 28,* 39–63. *26, 33, 35, 63*

SARNOFF, I., KATZ, D., and MCCLINTOCK, C., 1954. Attitude-change procedures and motivating patterns. In *Public opinion and propaganda*, eds. D. Katz, D. Cartwright, S. Eldersveld, and A. McC. Lee. New York, Dryden, 305–12. *52, 217, 223*

SCHANCK, R. L., 1932. A study of a community and its groups and institutions conceived of as behavior of individuals. *Psychol. Monogr., 43,* No. 2 (Whole No. 195). *6*

SEARS, R. R. and HOVLAND, C. I., 1941. Experiments on motor conflict. II.

Determination of mode of resolution by comparative strengths of conflicting responses. *J. exp. Psychol.*, *28*, 280–6. *215*

SELLS, S. B., 1936. The atmosphere effect: an experimental study of reasoning. *Arch. Psychol.*, No. 200. *100*

SIEGAL, S., 1956. *Nonparametric statistics for the behavioral sciences.* New York, McGraw-Hill. *44*

SMITH, M. B., 1949. Personal values as determinants of a political attitude. *J. Psychol.*, *28*, 477–86. *5, 16, 51*

SMITH, M. B., BRUNER, J. S., and WHITE, R. W., 1956. *Opinions and personality.* New York, Wiley. *7, 17, 52, 161, 217, 223*

STATTS, A. W. and STATTS, C. K., 1958. Attitudes established by classical conditioning. *J. Abnorm. Soc. Psychol.*, *57*, 37–40. *6*

STATTS, A. W. and STATTS, C. K., 1959. Meaning and *m:* correlated but separate. *Psychol. Rev.*, *66*, 136–44. *6*

STOTLAND, E., KATZ, D., and PATCHEN, M. The reduction of prejudice through the arousal of self-insight. *J. Pers.*, 1959, *27*, 507–31. *91*

STOUFFER, S. A., 1931. Experimental comparison of a statistical and a case history technique of attitude research. *Amer. Sociol. Soc. Proceedings*, *25*, 154–6. *7*

SUMNER, W. G., 1907. *Folkways.* Boston, Ginn. *65, 221*

TAGIURI, R. and PETRULLO, L., 1958. *Person perception and interpersonal behavior.* Stanford, Stanford University Press. *115*

THISTLETHWAITE, D., 1950. Attitude and structure as factors in the distortion of reasoning. *J. Abnorm. Soc. Psychol.*, *45*, 442–58. *66, 71, 99*

THURSTONE, L. L., 1929. Theory of attitude measurement. *Psychol. Rev.*, *36*, 222–41. *5*

TOLMAN, E. C., 1951. A psychological model. In *Toward a general theory of action*, eds. T. Parsons and E. A. Shils. Cambridge, Harvard University Press, 279–361. *5, 16*

WHITE, R. K., 1951. Value analysis: the nature and use of the method. Society for the Psychological Study of Social Issues. *19*

WILKINS, MINNA C., 1928. The effect of changed material on ability to do formal syllogistic reasoning. *Arch. Psychol.*, No. 102. *100f.*

WOODRUFF, A. D., 1942. Personal values and the direction of behavior. *Sch. Rev.*, *50*, 32–42. *5, 16, 51*

WOODRUFF, A. D., and DiVESTA, F. J., 1948. The relationship between values, concepts, and attitudes. *Educ. Psychol. Measmt.*, *8*, 645–60. *10, 16f., 24, 51*

WOODWORTH, R. S. and SELLS, S. B., 1935. An atmosphere effect in formal syllogistic reasoning. *J. Exper. Psychol.*, *18*, 451–60. *66, 100*

ZAJONC, R. B., 1955. Cognitive structure and cognitive tuning. Unpublished doctoral dissertation, University of Michigan. *161*